OFF THE BEATEN PATH® SERIES

Off the
SECOND EDITION
Beaten Path®

san francisco

A GUIDE TO UNIQUE PLACES

MICHAEL PETROCELLI

revised and updated by
Maxine Cass

INSIDERS' GUIDE®

GUILFORD, CONNECTICUT
AN IMPRINT OF THE GLOBE PEQUOT PRESS

The prices, rates, and hours listed in this guidebook
were confirmed at press time. We recommend,
however, that you call establishments to obtain
current information before traveling.

To buy books in quantity for corporate use
or incentives, call **(800) 962–0973, ext. 4551,**
or e-mail **premiums@GlobePequot.com.**

INSIDERS' GUIDE®

Copyright © 2003, 2005 by The Globe Pequot Press

Text design by Linda Loiewski
Maps created by Equator Graphics © The Globe Pequot Press
Illustrations by Carole Drong
Spot photography throughout © Maxine Cass

ISSN 1540-9325
ISBN 0-7627-3469-8

Manufactured in the United States of America
Second Edition/First Printing

To Mary Ellen for her art, vision, humor and courage,
Virginia for her native daughter's passion,
native son Ben for generously spanning cultures,
and in memory of David, who embraced his
adopted city in all its freedom and beauty.

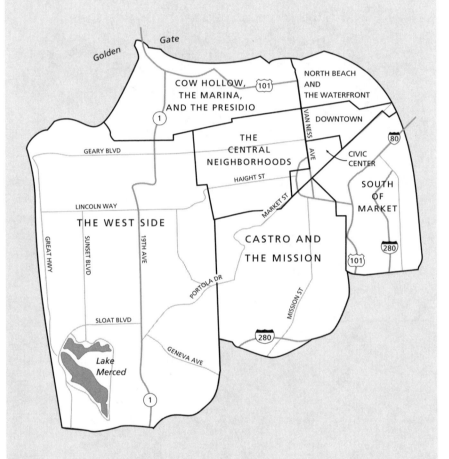

Golden   Gate

COW HOLLOW,   101   NORTH BEACH
THE MARINA,   AND
AND THE PRESIDIO   THE WATERFRONT

1   DOWNTOWN

GEARY BLVD   THE   80
              CENTRAL
              NEIGHBORHOODS   CIVIC
                               CENTER   SOUTH
              HAIGHT ST   OF
                                         MARKET

LINCOLN WAY

THE WEST SIDE

CASTRO AND   280
THE MISSION   101

PORTOLA DR

SLOAT BLVD

GENEVA AVE   280

Lake
Merced

VAN NESS AVE
MARKET ST
GREAT HWY
SUNSET BLVD
19TH AVE
MISSION ST

1

Contents

Acknowledgments vi

Introduction vii

Civic Center 1

Downtown 17

North Beach and the Waterfront 35

Cow Hollow, the Marina, and the Presidio 53

The West Side 69

The Central Neighborhoods 87

The Castro and the Mission 103

South of Market 119

Appendix 133

Indexes 135

    General Index 135

    Restaurants 138

    Lodgings 139

About the Authors 140

Acknowledgments

Thank you to the San Francisco Convention and Visitors Bureau, City Guides, and Al Baccari from the Fisherman's Wharf Merchants Association for helping me find the hidden gems in this city of many admirers. Thanks also to all of my friends who shared their secret spots and who didn't mock me when I took notes in restaurants.

—*Michael Petrocelli*

The mark of a dynamic city is how much it can change very quickly. Laurie Armstrong of the San Francisco Convention and Visitors Bureau cheerfully provided current information on major attractions. My friends Nancy Hoyt Belcher, Molly Cahill, Joan Kureczka, and native San Franciscan Virginia McCarthy shared their passion for this city by mining the subtle nuances they have discovered. Thanks also to Fred Gebhart, who is always ready to enjoy the pleasures of our city with me.

—*Maxine Cass*

Introduction

One of San Francisco's local newscasts advertises its program as news for "The Best Place on Earth," and no one in town seems to regard it as boasting. This is a city that likes itself. A lot. And why not? The temperature rarely goes below 50 or above 80 degrees, and it never snows. All forms of culture, high and low, are available year-round. San Francisco has long been home to communities of artists, writers, musicians, and designers creating new trends that spread across the country. And it is famously laid-back, eschewing a traditional marathon for a race in which everyone wears ridiculous costumes and nobody cares who wins.

Above all, San Francisco is a city of neighborhoods, many created by the dramatic geography, each with a unique culture. The city has always been shaped by new arrivals with differing experiences and sensibilities, and each of these groups has made its own San Francisco. There are the old and new arrivals of Chinatown, the gay and lesbian denizens of the Castro, the aging hippies of the Haight-Ashbury, the Mexican and Latin-American immigrants of the Mission, and the wealthy descendents of railroad barons on Nob Hill, making a trip through San Francisco like looking through a kaleidoscope of cultures while going back in time.

Many of these groups can be seen near the main tourist locations, but to really get a sense of the place, you have to plunge into the neighborhoods. Visit each area's main street: Eat a taco on Mission, drink a cappuccino on Columbus, and comb the secondhand stores on Fillmore. This is the meaning of "Off the Beaten Path" in San Francisco.

History

In 1848 San Francisco was nothing much to speak of: essentially a Spanish mission, a presidio, and a few houses in a picturesque but extremely remote location. There simply wasn't much there to convince easterners to ride across the continent in a wagon, set sail around Cape Horn, or venture a trip across the malarial isthmus of Panama. As hellish as those journeys were, however, people quickly signed up for them by the thousands when the news from California reached the East that year: Gold had been discovered.

In 1847 San Francisco had fewer than 500 residents. Midway through 1849 the population was 5,000, and by year's end it was 20,000. The gold began to run low during the 1850s, but people kept coming. As the decade reached a close, some 50,000 people called San Francisco home, roughly one hundred times the population before the discovery of gold. This tiny Spanish village was not well equipped to accept the large numbers of people, and with the overwhelming number of the newcomers being men, lawlessness reigned. The streets of the Barbary Coast, populated mostly by sailors, prostitutes, and other nonsociety types, became notorious crime centers, and the lack of an established police force led to the reign of vigilantes.

The veins of gold in the Sierra Nevada dried up before most could get their hands on a pile, but two watershed events at the end of the next two decades kept the people coming and removed any chance of San Francisco becoming a ghost town. The first came in 1859 with the discovery of silver in California and Nevada. Although none was found in San Francisco, the city's position by such a hospitable bay made it a natural place for embarkation and commerce. In both mining booms, most people made their fortunes not from unearthing precious metals, but from providing expensive goods and services to those who did. Then, in 1869, Leland Stanford and his fellow investors drove the golden spike in Promontory, Utah, to complete the first transcontinental railroad. Suddenly, San Francisco's relationship with the rest of the country changed. Rather than requiring a life-threatening trip of more than a month, coming to San Francisco consisted of a relatively comfortable ride of less than two weeks. Promises of instant fortune were no longer necessary to attract people to San Francisco. Instead, they could come for the weather or the lifestyle.

The fourth major event in San Francisco's early history was in 1906, when a devastating earthquake and the resulting fires ravaged the city, destroying 28,000 buildings and leaving tens of thousands of people homeless. With such widespread destruction, many around the country believed San Francisco would be wiped off the map, and many hoped it would be so, as punishment for its libertine ways. But San Francisco, whose symbol is a phoenix rising from the flames, had recovered from disasters before and did so once again. By the time it showed itself off by holding a world's fair in 1915, the turnaround was enough for President William Howard Taft to dub it "The City That Knows How."

Its trial by fire behind it, San Francisco grew prosperous once again, still attracting people from all over looking for a new start. The growth of Los Angeles took away San Francisco's status of capital of the West Coast, but the "City by the Bay" still held people's imaginations. Whether home to bohemians and beatniks in the 1950s, hippies in the 1960s, technology entrepreneurs in the 1990s, or, in 2004, being the first U.S. city to authorize lesbian and gay civil marriage, San Francisco has thrived on its reputation of acceptance—a place where new ways of thinking would be allowed to blossom.

Getting Around

Visitors, especially those who have just come from sprawling Los Angeles, will find San Francisco pleasingly compact. The city of about 750,000 people sits on a roughly square plot of 7 miles by 7 miles at the tip of a peninsula. It is bounded by the San Francisco Bay to the east and north, the Pacific Ocean to the west, and the cities of Brisbane and Daly City to the south. The streets mostly follow a grid system, quite an accomplishment given the many steep hills that planners had to deal with. Two important streets defy the right angles. Columbus Avenue cuts a diagonal through the neighborhood of North Beach, but leaves the grid unmolested. Market Street, the city's main drag, effectively puts an end to the grid north of it and starts a new, slightly askew one to its south.

On the West Side, in the Richmond and Sunset neighborhoods, the grid is especially easy to navigate. East-west streets, with a few exceptions, carry alphabetical names, starting with Anza Street in the north and ending with Wawona Street in the south. Numbered avenues, running north-south, get higher as you approach the beach, ending with 48th Avenue (although 13th Avenue has been superstitiously replaced by Funston Street). Confusingly, San Francisco also has a set of numbered *streets* in the southeastern part of the city hemmed in by Market Street. Be careful when being told an address on "24th," for example: Confirm whether it is a street or an avenue, or you could end up several miles from your destination and sorely disappointed.

Transportation

Although having a car can be useful for reaching some of the more remote parts of the city and the outlying areas, it will often be more of a nuisance than a help. The city is relatively small, and it typically takes more time to find reasonably priced parking than it does to drive to the most popular areas. Add to this the sheer terror that the precipitous hills can induce in even the most experienced drivers—and San Franciscans' notorious affinity for red-light running—and most will be more than happy to use the many public transportation options.

The main transit organization is Muni (rhymes with puny), which is short for San Francisco Municipal Railway. In addition to its orange-and-white buses, Muni also runs a limited underground train, streetcars, and the ever popular cable cars. Muni appears to be improving after many years as a city joke, but the system, while serviceable and reasonably extensive, can still be unreliable. The basic rule with Muni is to allow twice as much time as you think you need and be pleasantly surprised if you arrive early. When your train inexplicably stops in a tunnel or your bus loses contact with its electric wires, marooning it in the middle of the street, you'll be glad you planned conservatively. Muni

routes, official timetables, route maps, a frequency guide, and up-to-date service problem reports are posted on www.sfmuni.com/routes/indxrout.htm. Muni
even offers telephone comfort, "trip planning with real people," to frustrated
riders. Call 673–6864 Monday through Friday 6:00 A.M. to 8:00 P.M. and weekends and holidays 8:00 A.M. to 6:00 P.M.

Muni Metro is a light rail system that mainly shuttles people between
downtown and the city's southern and western neighborhoods. There are five
Muni Metro lines, all of which serve underground stations along Market Street
and run as aboveground streetcars away from downtown. Each line is named
with a letter and the street or neighborhood it serves. Most local commuters
who catch the Muni Metro along Judah Street, for instance, will tell you they
take the "N-Judah" to work. A nifty Web site (www.nextbus.com) uses satellite
tracking to provide live updates on when to expect a Muni Metro train at a
given stop, an especially useful service at night. Muni Metro shuts down
between 1:00 and 5:00 A.M., when service is replaced by "Owl" buses.

An adjunct to this system that is particularly useful for visitors is the F-
Market and Wharves line of streetcars that runs aboveground from Castro and
17th Streets east on Market Street and along the waterfront to Fisherman's Wharf.
This recently rehabilitated line uses historic streetcars from other cities, including St. Louis, Cincinnati, and Milan, each painted in its original color.

Do not confuse the streetcars with the cable cars, the smaller trolleys that
rumble improbably up and over the daunting hills. What distinguishes the cable
cars is right there in the name: Rather than running electrically, the cars are
pulled along by a series of cables that constantly run under the streets during
operating hours. There are three cable car lines: the Powell-Hyde, going from
the Powell Street turnaround to Aquatic Park; the Powell-Mason, also starting
at Powell and Market but ending in the heart of Fisherman's Wharf on Taylor
Street, a few steps from Bay Street; and the California, which goes from the
corner of California and Market Streets west; to Van Ness Avenue. Besides the
fun of standing on the running board and hanging on for dear life during the
precarious climbs and descents, the cable cars can actually be a useful conveyance, although long lines during peak hours can be frustrating. To avoid
long lines, walk a few blocks up from the turnaround, board, and pay the fare.
A ride on a cable car costs $3.00 each way any time for anyone ages five or
older. Cable cars run from 6:00 A.M. to midnight. No transfers are accepted.
Except for rides on cable cars, Muni charges adults $1.25 for a ride, with trans-
fers good from ninety minutes to two hours.

If you will be relying on public transportation to get around, you will probably want to buy a Muni Passport. The pass allows unlimited rides on buses,
streetcars, Muni Metro, and cable cars. Passports are available in one-, three-,
and seven-day increments and must be used on consecutive days. They can be

bought at cable car turnarounds, the San Francisco Convention and Visitors Bureau Information Center at Halladie Plaza (below Market and Powell Streets), San Francisco International Airport (SFO), a few shops around town (check www.sfmuni.com/fares/fareinfo.htm#passports), or online at www.sfvisitor.org/cgi-bin/webc.exe/st_main.html. If you will be staying a while, you can buy a pass good for one calendar month at the convention and visitors bureau. One privately marketed option is San Francisco CityPass (http://citypass.net) that covers Muni and cable car rides, a bay cruise, and entrance to five museums over seven days. For attractions in and beyond San Francisco, another private company offers a one-, two-, three-, or five-day Go San Francisco Card (www.gosanfranciscocard.com).

Another system of more limited use within San Francisco is BART (Bay Area Rapid Transit). Although it's chiefly a regional rail system, BART's two stations under Mission Street can be convenient for travel within the city. BART also shares four Market Street stations with Muni Metro. Board BART at any of these six stations for direct service to the airport (SFO). The best resource for sorting out the various transit options for any journey is the *Official San Francisco Street and Transit Map,* available at bookstores, tourist offices, and some Muni Metro stations. The map covers BART, Muni, and other regional bus systems. Up-to-date public transportation information with routes, traffic flow data, bicycle routes, and maps for the entire San Francisco Bay Area is posted on http://transit.511.org.

Fees, Prices, and Rates

San Francisco's rents are among the highest in the country, and this can translate into high costs for tourists. Luckily, many of the attractions mentioned in this book won't cost you a penny, but the same cannot be said for meals and shelter.

For lodging purposes, a double room for less than $100 a night is considered inexpensive, $100 to $200 is moderate, and more than $200 is expensive.

In the case of restaurants, a full meal for less than $15 a person is inexpensive, $15 to $30 is moderate, and anything above $30 is expensive.

Area Code

San Francisco's sole area code is 415, and it does not need to be dialed within the city. Unless otherwise noted, all the phone numbers in this book can be reached with the 415 prefix.

Sources of Information

There are many good resources for up-to-date information on San Francisco, including:

The San Francisco Chronicle (www.sfgate.com/chronicle). The *Chronicle* is frequently the butt of jokes nationally, including a memorable quip by *Washington Post* editor Ben Bradlee in *All the President's Men*. At one point in the film, someone suggests to Bradlee (as played by Jason Robards) that the *Post* print yesterday's weather report for "people who were drunk or slept all day." Bradlee's response is "Send it out to the *San Francisco Chronicle*. They need it." Whether Bradlee ever said this in real life, the *Chronicle* has never quite lived it down. The opinions of other cities notwithstanding, it is the paper of record for this often self-involved city. The Sunday Datebook section, the baby pink, "Pinkie," or "Pink Sheet," is the bible for the upcoming week's entertainment options, including tours.

The San Francisco Bay Guardian (www.sfbg.com). The more venerable of the city's two free alternative weeklies, the *Guardian* seems to take skewering the *Chronicle* as a major part of its mission. It is a good source for updates on the week's more unusual entertainment options and left-wing politics. (Its annual mid-May list of Bay Area nude beaches is much perused.) You'll find the *Guardian* in black boxes all over the city and stacked up in cafes and bookstores.

SF Weekly (www.sfweekly.com). One of a chain of alternative U.S. city newspapers, it has a following of the youthful, in-your-face variety. The tabloid's rabble-rousing equals the *Guardian* in tone; they both publish "Best of..." lists once a year that point out the quirkiest best *and worst* things about the area's food, restaurants, bars, parks, dog-friendly venues, etc. The farther out, the better the write-up. Local yoga parlors, computer repair services, and the array of businesses in between hedge the bet by advertising in both papers, published on Wednesday. *SF Weekly* is found in red boxes citywide.

San Francisco. The monthly magazine, once published for the local public television station viewers, has gone mainstream with well-written features on the area, an arts summary, restaurant reviews, and profiles of local notables and corporations.

Among the number of useful online guides to this wired city are www .sfgate.com/traveler, www.bayarea.citysearch.com, and www.bayinsider.com.

Walking Tours

There are countless organizations offering good walking tours of San Francisco. They include:

City Guides. A nonprofit group loosely affiliated with the Public Library, City Guides offers free walking tours all over the city nearly every day of the year. Tours are led by volunteers, most of them retirees with long memories about the topics and areas they cover. Their schedule is packed with interesting programs year-round. Special experimental tours are offered in May and October. Check www.sfcityguides.org or call 557–4266, or e-mail tours@sfcity guides.org for the monthly schedule.

Friends of Recreation and Parks. These volunteers lead free tours of various areas in Golden Gate Park, usually on weekends. Among the offerings are "stroller walks" specially designed for people pushing smaller people around. Call 750–5105 or visit www.sfparks.org for more information.

Cruisin' the Castro. This group provides a great overview of gay and lesbian history and the unique neighborhood where so much of it has been made. Guide Trevor Hailey makes it fun for gays, lesbians, and those who practice what she calls "the alternate lifestyle." Call 550–8110 for more information.

Wok Wiz. Author Shirley Fong-Torres leads this group, which offers tours of Chinatown with an emphasis on eating. The tours teach history but center on stops in tea shops and food markets along the way. Walks end with a dim sum lunch. Evenings are ripe for Chinatown Ghost Walks or a History and Feng Shui Walking Tour. Call (650) 355–9657 or visit www.wokwiz.com for more information.

Victorian Home Walk. Harking back to the days when San Franciscans would rendezvous by the lobby clock, Jay Gifford's tour begins in the landmark Westin St. Francis Hotel's old lobby, off Powell Street. The walk and scenic trolley tour to several Victorian-packed neighborhoods takes in 200 or so "painted ladies," with a visit to a Queen Anne. Call 252–9485 or visit www.victorianwalk.com for more information.

Shove This in Your Suitcase

San Francisco has long been a great literary city, and the following books make fun and informative companions for the visitor.

The Joy Luck Club, by Amy Tan
Chinese mothers and their assimilated modern daughters intertwine in each other's stories, played out in the real alleys of San Francisco's Chinatown.

The Maltese Falcon, by Dashiell Hammett
For a look at downtown San Francisco in the 1920s, there is no better book. Hammett notes exactly where each event in the novel occurs, down to the street corners. And no character has ever been cooler than Sam Spade.

Tales of the City, by Armistead Maupin
Collected from a newspaper serial, it tells the story of 1970s San Francisco through the racy adventures of the residents of a Russian Hill street.

Daughter of Fortune, by Isabel Allende
The story of a young Chilean girl who comes to California paints a vivid picture of Gold Rush–era San Francisco.

Carter Beats the Devil, by Glen David Gold
A fun novel based on the true story of a magician who performed for President Warren G. Harding the night of his death at the Palace Hotel.

Baghdad by the Bay, by Herb Caen
A classic take on 1940s San Francisco by the late, legendary columnist for the *Chronicle.*

West from Home, by Laura Ingalls Wilder
A collection of letters the onetime pioneer girl wrote to her husband during her two-month visit to San Francisco in 1915 during the Panama Pacific International Exposition.

Don't Be That Guy

San Franciscans are generally very welcoming to tourists, happily offering directions and recommending places to visit, eat, and go out—with or without being asked. Many seem to get a guilty glee, however, from watching the uninitiated contend with the city's unusual weather patterns. In order to avoid getting laughed at—and being miserable—keep a few things in mind and pack accordingly.

First, San Francisco summers are unlike those almost anywhere else. The traditional summer months of July and August are often the most persistently foggy and can be cold enough for a heavy jacket. October and November, however, are generally glorious, with sunshine all day and temperatures nearing 80 degrees.

Second, San Francisco is a city of microclimates. The hills and valleys create an environment such that one neighborhood can be sunny and warm while another is socked in with fog and freezing. Later in the day, the opposite will be true. What this means is even if it is sunny where you are staying, carry a sweater or a jacket when you go out for the day, and wear shorts only at your peril.

I Want to Ride My Bicycle

Despite the hilly terrain, bike riding is a hugely popular activity in San Francisco, and cyclists make up a potent political lobby. One Friday night a month, the city's more activist pedal-pushers take part in Critical Mass, part Tour de San Francisco and part peaceful protest. Starting downtown right around the evening rush hour, thousands of riders move en masse about the city, closing down streets and further snarling the already hideous traffic.

Cycling is also a great way to enjoy the city, but choose your routes carefully so as not to find your legs turning to jelly on a steep incline. Below are a few of the easiest and most scenic routes. For more specific information on cycling, pick up the *San Francisco Bike Map & Walking Guide* (available at bookstores and bike rental shops), which gives the percent grade of every block in the city, or visit www.bicycle.sfgov.org/site/uploadedfiles/dpt/bike /SFBikeMap2002.pdf.

Along the Waterfront (Easy). An almost completely flat route takes you from the Ferry Building along The Embarcadero, past Fisherman's Wharf and the Marina, all the way to Fort Point and the Golden Gate Bridge, 15 miles round-trip.

Golden Gate Park (Moderate). Begin at the park's eastern end, near Haight Street, and cruise to the beach and back. There are a few ups and downs along the way, but nothing too rough, 8 miles round-trip.

The Beach (Moderate). Start at Fort Funston in the city's southwest corner, and cruise north on Skyline Boulevard, joining up with Great Highway for a mellow ride along Ocean Beach, 10 miles round-trip.

A few things to keep in mind while cycling:

- Be very careful when riding on city streets; look both ways even when you have a green light. San Francisco drivers are notorious for blowing through red lights.
- Bikes are allowed on ferries from Marin County. This means that you can ride across the Golden Gate Bridge and down the steep hill into the picturesque town of Sausalito without fear of the climb back up. Enjoy a meal on the bay and catch a ride back to the Ferry Building with ease. Call 923–2000 or visit www.goldengateferry.org/services/ bikes.html for schedules.
- Bikes are not allowed on the Bay Bridge to Oakland and Berkeley. You can, however, bring your bike on BART, which serves both cities. During weekday rush hour periods, bikes enter and exit at specific stations (visit www.bart.gov/guide/bikes/bikerules.asp) and may accompany owners anywhere except in the BART train's first car.

Calendar of Events

JANUARY

San Francisco International Art Exposition. More than one hundred galleries exhibit works at Fort Mason. Call (877) 734–2399 or visit www.sfiae.com.

FEBRUARY

Chinese New Year. Don't miss the glimmering golden dragon dancing down Market Street to Union Square, preceded by floats, the year's Chinese zodiac animal, and hundreds of fringe-mane lions, dancers, and marching bands. Call 391–9680 or visit www.chineseparade.com.

Pacific Orchid Exposition. Shop for rare species of the fragrant plant or just marvel at the people who are obsessed with them. Call 665–2468 or visit www.orchidsanfrancisco.org.

Russian Festival. Dancing, food, and community are featured at the Russian Center of San Francisco, 2450 Sutter Street. Call 921–7631 or visit www.russian centersf.com.

San Francisco Tribal, Folk, and Textile Art Show. Eighty galleries exhibit and sell high quality pre-1940s ethnic artwork at Fort Mason. Call (310) 455–2886 or visit www.caseylees.com.

Tulipmania. More than 39,000 tulips are on display at Pier 39. Call 705–5000 or visit www.pier39.com.

MARCH

San Francisco Asian American Film Festival. Where better to get a feel for the culture of one-quarter of San Francisco's population than at cinemas around the area and in Japantown? Call 863–0814 or 865–1588 or visit www.naata net.org/festival.

St. Patrick's Day Parade. Starting around noon on the weekend closest to March 17, the green goes up Market Street to City Hall. Call 675–9885 or visit www.sfstpatricksdayparade.com.

APRIL

Japanese Cherry Blossom Festival. A Japantown street fair, parade, and taiko (drumming) demonstration over two weekends. Call 563–2313 or visit www .nccbf.org.

Opening Day on the Bay. Watch from the Marina as decorated classic and modern boats parade along the waterfront. Visit www.picya.org/News/Open ing_Day/index.html.

Saint Stupid's Day Parade. Winding through the Financial District on April Fool's Day, costumed marchers "disorganized" by the First Church of the Last

Laugh honor the patron of parking meters. Call (510) 841–1898 or visit www .saintstupid.com.

San Francisco International Film Festival. Two hundred films are shown over two weeks at theaters around the city. Call 561–5000 or visit www.sffs.org.

MAY

Bay to Breakers. May be the quintessential San Francisco event, when costumed and half-naked revelers, along with a few serious athletes, run the 12K course from The Embarcadero to the beach. Call 359–2800 or visit www.bayto breakers.com.

Black and White Ball. The black-tie benefit in odd-numbered years for the San Francisco Symphony brings out anyone who's anyone. Call 503–5509 or visit www.bwball.com.

Carnaval. The parade and glorified Mission District street party on Memorial Day weekend pays homage to Latino roots, but costumes, music, dance, and revelers span the ethnic gamut. Call 920–0125 or visit www.carnavalsf.com.

Cinco de Mayo Festival. A parade down Mission Street and a party in Parque de los Niños, 23rd and Folsom Streets at Treat Avenue, celebrate the Mexican victory over French forces in 1862.

JUNE

Escape from Alcatraz Triathlon. In-shape crazies jump off a ferry near Alcatraz Island to swim, bike, and run themselves into exhaustion. Call (831) 373–0678 or visit www.tricalifornia.com.

Haight-Ashbury Street Fair. A celebration of this neighborhood's legendary past. Call 863–3489 or visit www.haightstreetfair.org.

North Beach Festival. Poetry readings, street chalking, animal blessing, pizza tossing, and lots and lots of food. Call 989–2220 or visit www.sfnorthbeach .org/festival.

San Francisco International Lesbian and Gay Film Festival. Call 703–8650 or visit www.frameline.org/festival.

San Francisco Lesbian, Gay, Bisexual, Transgender Pride Parade (Gay Pride Parade). San Franciscans of all lifestyle persuasions line Market Street to watch Dykes on Bikes traditionally motor up the start of a long procession of marchers for causes and humorous send-ups of nuns—in drag—and scorn for many political candidates. Call 864–3733 or visit www.sfpride.org.

JULY

Books by the Bay. Author readings and tables from area independent bookstores in Yerba Buena Gardens. Visit www.booksbythebay.com.

Fillmore Street Jazz Festival. Free jazz on one of the city's nicest streets. Call (800) 731–0003 or visit www.fillmorestreetjazzfest.com.

San Francisco Jewish Film Festival. The first Jewish film festival in the world includes screenings at the historic Castro Theatre. Call 621–0556 or visit www.sfjff.com.

AUGUST

Nihonmachi Street Fair. The celebration of Asian and Pacific-Islander cultures takes place in Japantown. Call 771–9861 or visit www.nihonmachistreet fair.org.

SEPTEMBER

Cable Car Bell-Ringing Competition. At Union Square, gripmen are judged on their creativity and originality in sounding the chime. Call 923–6217 or visit www.sfmuni.com.

Comedy Day. Top comedians, including Robin Williams and Whoopi Goldberg, have entertained giggling, guffawing masses for free in Golden Gate Park for a quarter century. Visit www.comedyday.com.

San Francisco Blues Festival. Local and national acts perform outdoors at Fort Mason. Call 979–5588 or visit www.sfblues.com.

San Francisco Shakespeare Festival. Free performances in Golden Gate Park. Call 865–4434 or visit www.sfshakes.org.

OCTOBER

Castro Street Fair. A celebration of gay culture in the historic neighborhood. Call 841–1824 or visit www.castrostreetfair.org.

Exotic Erotic Ball. Not for the kids, this annual masquerade ball. Call 567–2255 or visit www.exoticeroticball.com.

Fleet Week. Tour naval ships, watch the Parade of Ships, and marvel at the airshow near the Golden Gate Bridge. Call 705–5500.

San Francisco Jazz Festival. The two-week October through November event at venues around the city attracts some of the best in the field. Call 398–5655 or visit www.sfjazz.org.

NOVEMBER

Run to the Far Side. A 10K run in the spirit of Gary Larson's cartoons. Call 321–8124 or visit www.calacademy.org.

DECEMBER

Sing-It-Yourself Messiah. Experienced vocalists and novice warblers combine their efforts on Handel's masterpiece at Davies Symphony Hall. Call 759–3475 or visit www.sfcm.edu.

Civic Center

Following the 1906 earthquake and a doomed previous attempt, city planners decided to build a center of San Francisco officialdom and culture, and they wanted to go big. Despite the natural disaster, San Francisco was still a city with worldly pretensions, so planners decided to create a civic center that would make the city look more like Paris. This meant classical buildings—preferably built by men who had studied at the École des Beaux-Arts in Paris—and wide squares with geometrically arranged trees. The result is an attractive area with the biggest collection of Beaux Arts buildings in the United States outside of Washington, D.C. The Civic Center and its surrounding areas are also a study in contrasts, as the center of arts and government is right next to the Tenderloin, one of the poorest areas of the city, and Hayes Valley, one of the most up and coming.

The natural reaction to seeing *City Hall* (1 Dr. Carlton B. Goodlett Place) for the first time is, "I didn't know San Francisco was the capital of California." It's not, and the good people of Sacramento would rather you didn't forget, but you could be fooled because the building is so grand and that dome is so darn big. It's not only bigger than the one on the State Capitol, but also bigger than the one on the United States Capitol. At 306 feet, it is the fifth tallest dome in the world,

CIVIC CENTER

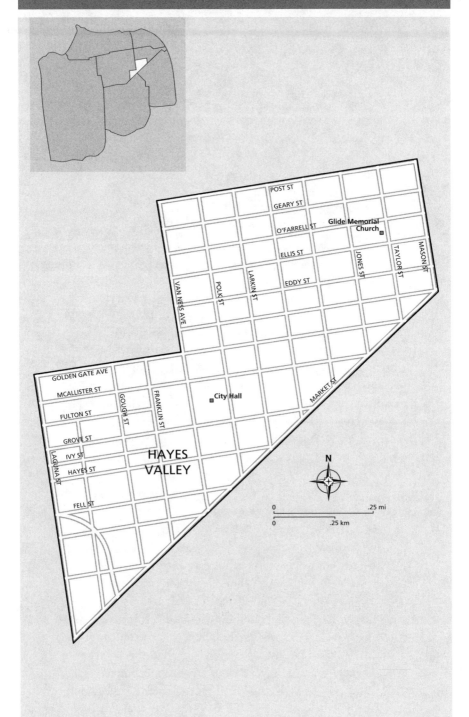

POST ST

GEARY ST

O'FARRELL ST

Glide Memorial Church

ELLIS ST

EDDY ST

VAN NESS AVE

POLK ST

LARKIN ST

JONES ST

TAYLOR ST

MASON ST

GOLDEN GATE AVE

MCALLISTER ST

FULTON ST

GROVE ST

IVY ST

HAYES ST

FELL ST

LAGUNA ST

GOUGH ST

FRANKLIN ST

City Hall

MARKET ST

HAYES VALLEY

N

0 .25 mi

0 .25 km

behind such notable structures as St. Peter's Basilica in Rome and the Duomo in Florence. The one where Congress meets is only 287 feet tall. Two blocks wide and one block deep, City Hall encompasses an area of more than 500,000 square feet.

The building you see today is actually the second City Hall to stand on this spot. The first also sported a large dome in the Beaux Arts style, but it was riddled by corruption and mismanagement even before the politicians took up residence. Crews broke ground on the new site in 1872, intending to finish up in four years and spend $1.5 million. Twenty-seven years and some $6 million later, it actually opened for business, amid accusations of corruption and graft.

The new building was not quite as elegant as many had hoped, according to a report at the time by the superintendent of buildings: "On taking possession of City Hall we found it in a most dilapidated condition and so filthy as to be almost beyond description." He went on to list eleven of the more egregious problems, among them: "the water closets and toilet rooms throughout the building were so unsanitary that the occupants of the building who had any regard for their health would not use them . . ." and "the plastering in all of the corridors and in many of the rooms looked very much as if some person or persons had deliberately tried to remove it from the walls with a hatchet." Attractiveness and comfort had apparently not been sacrificed to ensure the structural integrity of building either, because on April 18, 1906, the Great Earthquake shook it to the ground. It took twenty-seven years to build and twenty-eight seconds to collapse.

After this disaster, San Franciscans were understandably reluctant to shell out for a new City Hall, but by 1911, a new, popular mayor was elected, and the city's mood had changed. James "Sunny Jim" Rolph—an optimist, as his moniker suggests—made rebuilding City Hall a top priority. After getting an $8.8 million bond past voters, Rolph set out to look for an architect. Rolph had three requirements for the designer of the new building. He had to be an engineer, to protect against future earthquakes; he had to have studied in Paris, as was the architectural snobbery of the day; and he had to have an office in San

TOP ATTRACTIONS NEAR THE CIVIC CENTER

City Hall	Asian Art Museum
San Francisco Public Library	Glide Memorial Church
Veterans Building	

City Hall

Francisco, presumably so the mayor could storm into his chambers and throttle him if the thing were to collapse again.

The winning bidder, Arthur Brown of the local firm Bakewell and Brown, met all of the requirements and submitted a design modeled after the Les Invalides complex in Paris. He also impressed Rolph with his plan to make the dome 20 feet higher than the U.S. Capitol, a fact that the mayor liked to brag about later. Rolph, who would serve as mayor for nineteen years and die as governor of California, broke ground on the site himself in 1913. This time, construction went smoothly, and Rolph dedicated it two and a half years later. On the side facing Civic Center Plaza, above the main entrance, is the Mayor's Balcony. In the days before radio, Rolph liked to address the people from his spot high above the plaza, shouting at the top of his lungs, one has to imagine.

While in the rotunda, you will almost certainly come upon a bride and groom, in full regalia, posing for pictures on the dramatic marble staircase. In 1954, City Hall played host to one of the country's most fabled if ill-fated weddings when local legend Joe DiMaggio married Marilyn Monroe. The pair tried to keep the nuptials a secret, but about 500 fans and every reporter in town got wind of the wedding and jammed the judge's chambers. His Honor tossed everyone out for the ceremony, but the newlyweds had to sneak and push their way out of the building and into their waiting car. The *Chronicle* capped its report on the scene with a quote from the wistful presiding judge: "I forgot to kiss the bride."

Along the rotunda's south wall is what looks like a rubber sandwich, about a foot of rubber in between two metal plates. This is one of the "base isolators" that were placed under the building's foundation after the 1989 earthquake. These and a 4-foot moat around City Hall provide some separation between the building and the earth, allowing it to sway freely from side to side rather than be subjected to the earth's violent motions. Although the 1989 temblor didn't have the same disastrous impact on City Hall as the one in 1906 did, it caused enough damage that engineers needed to come up with this new plan. The quake caused the dome to twist 2 inches on its frame in a corkscrew motion and left cracks in the floors and walls.

Renovations began in 1995 and encompassed more than just earthquake retrofitting. The original dome was gilded with copper, which had turned green over the years. San Franciscans were used to seeing a green and black dome, but renovators restored it to its original golden color for City Hall's 1999 reopening. This color is echoed all around the building, providing a striking contrast to the white facade.

The rotunda is flanked by two "light courts," named for the natural light that flows in through their glass ceilings. During World War II, these skylights were tarred over to foil enemy bombers that might fly overhead, and were only uncovered during the 1995 renovations. The North Light Court holds a gift shop and cafe. In February 2004, City Hall officers, acting on authorization from Mayor Gavin Newsom, issued marriage licenses to gay and lesbian couples, many of whom were married at City Hall. The rotunda staircase became the venue for wedding pictures that were broadcast around the world. More than 4,000 same-sex marriages were performed before the California Supreme Court froze the nuptial activity a month later.

City Hall is open Monday through Friday 8:00 A.M. to 8:00 P.M. and Saturday noon to 4:00 P.M.; closed holidays. Call 554–6023 for information on free historical guided tours, offered Tuesday through Saturday.

Across Civic Center Plaza to the east is the 1996 ***San Francisco Public Library*** (100 Larkin Street). The place is gorgeous, with wide lobbies, an 80-foot-high atrium, plenty of study carrels, and lots of computers, but there is, at first glance, something missing: books. In most cases, the books are tucked

AUTHORS' FAVORITES NEAR THE CIVIC CENTER

City Hall	Glide Memorial Church on a Sunday
Hayes Street in Hayes Valley	Edinburgh Castle

away in stacks out of sight; you have to ask a library page to fetch one for you. This makes the whole place feel almost like a museum, but it does have some very nice features. The Fisher Children's Center on the second floor actually has some books on display, along with a collection of rare editions of children's literature, including *Alice's Adventures in Wonderland.* Other rooms include an African-American history center and a Filipino-American center on the third floor, and a Bay Area Art, Music, Dance, Theater and Film Center on the floor above. Call 557–4400 or visit http://sfpl.org for more information.

Just to the library's north is the building that was the old public library. The **Asian Art Museum** (200 Larkin Street) moved from Golden Gate Park in 2003 in a novel use of one of Civic Center's 1917 Beaux Arts buildings. A sky-lit courtyard was designed by Italian architect Gae Aulenti, best known for another innovative redesign of a cavernous railway station—Paris's Musée d'Orsay. The heart and soul of the galleries are softly lit Asian and Southeast Asian collections, arranged geographically to emphasize the art, skilled artisans, and the media they used, and the religions that influenced the East. With 15,000 objects, the Asian, as it's known, has the largest U.S. collection of Asian artifacts to draw from and displays 3,000 pieces each year. Changing exhibitions dominate the ground floor.

The Asian Art Museum could be tediously comprehensive. Instead it is organized along three themes: Buddhism, the strongest collections and center of most Asian culture; trade and cultural exchange, which with prosperity spread beliefs throughout the region; and objects of local belief that influenced everything from ceramic pot decoration to puppets. Rare Tibetan scrolls, Sikh art, 832 Japanese bamboo baskets, the largest collection of Korean art outside Korea, and supremely serene Buddhas create an oasis within San Francisco's government core. Open Tuesday through Sunday 10:00 A.M. to 5:00 P.M., with half-price admission and extended hours Thursday until 9:00 P.M. Admission is $10.00 for adults, $7.00 for seniors, $6.00 for college students and children ages thirteen to seventeen. The first Tuesday of the month is free. Call 581–3500 or visit www.asianart.org for more information.

Directly opposite City Hall to the west, across Van Ness Avenue, are the twin buildings of the **San Francisco War Memorial.** Soon after the end of World War I, returning veterans began a campaign for a building and an auditorium commemorating their efforts. At the same time, city leaders were drawing up plans for a cultural center featuring an opera house, symphony hall, and art museum near the new City Hall. The two proposals were combined, and after more than a decade of fund-raising and politicking, the efforts came to fruition in 1932 with the **War Memorial Complex.** The complex consists of two buildings, nearly indistinguishable from each other architecturally, on

Naked Ambition

Over the years, just about every San Francisco mayor has been accused of being dirty, but only one managed to find trouble while getting clean.

In 1995, about a week before Election Day, Mayor Frank Jordan was locked in a tight reelection battle with State Assembly Speaker Willie Brown, and he apparently felt he needed to do something to shake his boring image. The solution? He invited two Los Angeles DJs into his house, figuring he'd play along and show them he was a good sport. The two DJs, broadcasting live, told the mayor that they had taken a poll to see what voters wanted from the mayor: "Over 25,000 said they would pull the lever if you would disrobe, lather up, and shower with us." Inexplicably, he agreed, and the three men hopped in.

Boring was the least-used adjective San Franciscans uttered when they picked up their afternoon papers to find a picture of the naked mayor, cropped just above the line of propriety, yucking it up in the shower with the two radio personalities. Whether it was disgust or something more substantive that motivated voters, Jordan's gambit failed, and Brown was elected. Jordan was unrepentant when talking to reporters after the incident. "It shows two things very clearly," he said. "One, I've got nothing to hide, and two, I'm squeaky clean."

opposite sides of a courtyard. Bakewell and Brown, who had a hit on their hands with City Hall, were also chosen for this new endeavor, and they designed it to complement the first project. The buildings' heights are roughly the same as that of City Hall (minus the dome), and the same classic Beaux Arts style was observed.

In addition to remaining important cultural centers for the city, an important international treaty was signed at each of the buildings. On the north side of the courtyard is the *Veterans Building* (401 Van Ness Avenue), where most of the meetings and ceremonies that resulted in the United Nations charter were held. The main feature of the Veterans Building is *Herbst Theater,* an auditorium hosting musical events and a lecture series. The murals that adorn the theater's walls are leftovers from San Francisco's world's fair, the 1915 Panama Pacific International Exposition. They were painted by Frank Brangwyn, a Belgian painter who lived in England. All the artists hired for the fair agreed to come to San Francisco to paint simultaneously in the same studio, because the planners hoped they would be inspired by the other artists' choices of color, leading to a more coherent collection. Brangwyn, the only non-American commissioned, agreed to this, but he never came to America, not then or ever in his life. Not only did he never see his paintings hanging in the Palace of Abundance, he never saw them in their entirety because the 18-by-25-foot canvases were too large for his studio. Instead, he had to roll up one section in order to work on the others. The eight panels, grouped in four pairs, represent the four elements. Call the Herbst Theater at 621–6600 for performance schedules and ticket information or check http://sfwmpac.org.

The other half of the complex is the **War Memorial Opera House** (301 Van Ness Avenue), just across a gated courtyard from the Veterans Building.

itcouldhavebeen worse

Until March 12, 2003, the much hated Central Freeway went only as far as Fell Street, before disgorging cars onto surface roads. It was an eyesore, sure, but nothing compared to two decades ago when it went eight blocks farther north and plagued the entire neighborhood with its shadows. As grateful as Hayes Valley residents are to have the monster pruned back, the whole city should be relieved that a 1960s plan was not enacted. It called for the freeway to split into two branches, each of which would snake through northern neighborhoods, all the way to the Golden Gate Bridge. Community activists fought and stopped the measure, and they are owed a debt of gratitude. In 2006 a new ramp will dump thousands of commuters at Market Street, while Octavia Street expands to boulevard width with a landscaped meridian. Not bad for one of San Francisco's grayest and most awkward eyesores.

San Francisco had long been a city that loved opera. Most of the productions were on a small scale, though, staged mostly in theaters in the predominantly Italian North Beach neighborhood. By 1919, with spirits soaring in the once disaster-ravaged city, the city's bigwigs were ready to build a theater to stage opera on a grand scale. The San Francisco Opera Company was incorporated in 1923, but, still having no house of its own, held its performances in the nearby Civic Auditorium. Difficulties raising the necessary funds, acquiring suitable land, and satisfying the ambitions of both the arts leaders and the veterans groups delayed the beginning of construction until 1931, and the first aria was not belted out on its stage until October 15, 1932. The production that evening was Giacomo Puccini's *Tosca*. The opening line, "Finalmente!" (finally!) reportedly was met with riotous, knowing laughter from the audience.

It must have been worth the wait, stunning as it is. Before even entering the hall, theatergoers pass through a vast marble-floored lobby and into a plush foyer, complete with Doric columns and a coffered ceiling. The hall itself is amazingly intimate, considering that it holds about one-and-a-half times as many people as the original Paris Opera House, which influenced the design. Four floors of seating are stacked above the orchestra level, in addition to twenty-five luxurious boxes, each with a private vestibule. The building did more than just look good: Bakewell and Brown incorporated the most advanced sound system the early 1930s could offer, and audiences were said to be stunned at the glorious sound. A writer for *Time* magazine, on hand for opening night, called it "easily the most attractive and practical building of its kind in the United States."

The Opera House's beauty was put to diplomatic use after World War II. After the negotiations in the Veterans Building, the United Nations charter was officially signed on the Opera House stage on June 26, 1945. To honor the historic occasion, the UN has held commemorative meetings in the Opera House on the tenth, twentieth, twenty-fifth, and fiftieth anniversaries. Its reputation as a site for diplomatic ceremonies thus cemented, the Opera House also hosted the signing of the San Francisco Peace Treaty in 1951, which officially ended hostilities between Japan and the United States. Dual opera seasons run September through December and June to July. Buy a ticket to any performance except an opera opening and you're entitled to a free half-hour lecture on the production by a local music expert. During the main season, docents conduct behind-the-scenes and architecture tours. Call (510) 524–5220. The San Francisco Ballet (http://sfballet.org) dances and pirouettes on the Opera House stage from February through April, with a much-beloved—and sold out—holiday season *Nutcracker.* Call 861–4008 for opera performances and ticket information or visit http://sfopera.com.

Across Grove Street from the Opera House is the War Memorial Complex's modern cousin, **Davies Symphony Hall** (201 Van Ness Avenue), built in 1980. The curved building with its jutting balconies and brilliant lighting might look oddly matched with the classical structures around it, but its height and cornice lines were actually designed to echo those of the others. Call 552–8000 or visit www.sfsymphony.org for San Francisco Symphony information.

West of the stately Civic Center, behind the temples of high culture, is **Hayes Valley,** a testament to urban renaissance and the good that can result from even the worst events. As recently as the 1980s, this section of the city, nestled west of Van Ness Avenue and north of Market Street, was forbidding territory where drug dealers and prostitutes constituted most of the retail activity. Their control of the streets was helped in no small part by the Central Freeway, a monstrous concrete overpass that cast intimidating shadows over these blocks. The earthquake of 1989, which collapsed a similar structure in Oakland with tragic results, rendered the Central Freeway unsound, and a big chunk of it was torn down. Its removal allowed light to flood in, and Hayes Valley began to sprout businesses the way a plant finally moved out of the shade sprouts flowers. Today, Hayes Valley is one of the city's best shopping districts and a sudden center of international hipness, with French, Italian, German, Belgian,

Brazilian, and African establishments thriving side by side. Perfectly positioned to serve both Civic Center employees and the pretheater crowd, Hayes Valley's unique galleries, boutiques, cafes, bars, and restaurants bustle day and night.

Most of the action in the area centers on Hayes Street, starting just across Franklin Street behind Davies Symphony Hall. On the left-hand side of this block is *Champ de Mars* (347 Hayes Street), a small shop cluttered with knickknacks and objets d'art straight from the streets of the City of Lights. In fact, this is the place to go if you desire a sign from a Paris street. You can even pick your favorite *arrondisement*. Imported from France by the store's Gallic proprietors, the goods make for an eclectic mix in the delightfully cluttered shop. Some items, like the metal signs to attach to the bathroom door, would be at home in the Arc de Triomphe gift shop, but the antique furniture and well-worn tricolors that look like they've survived a few trips to the barricades make this a browser's dream. Open Tuesday through Saturday 11:00 A.M. to 6:30 P.M., Sunday from noon to 5:00 P.M.; closed Monday. Call 252–9434.

Speaking of things Parisian, a few doors down is *Hayes and Vine Wine Bar* (377 Hayes Street), a popular spot pouring wines not only from France, but from Italy, Spain, South America, and California's Napa Valley as well. The small room's decor is simple and comfy—lots of exposed brick and cushy, plush seats—allowing the wine to take center stage. With more than 1,100 choices, ranging from the rare to the relatively pedestrian, both the connoisseur and the neophyte will be satisfied. You can order by the bottle or the glass, or try one of the weekly "flights" of similar wines for tasting. The atmosphere is mellow, and while the sommeliers know their wine, they won't mock you for confusing a Merlot with a Cabernet. Food is limited to hors d'oeuvres, including cheese, pâté, fois gras, and smoked fish, that complement the wines beautifully. Open Monday through Thursday 5:00 P.M. to midnight, Friday 5:00 P.M. to 1:00 A.M., Saturday 3:00 P.M. to 1:00 A.M., and Sunday 3:00 to 10:00 P.M. Call 626–5301. Moderate.

Veer right on Octavia to reach *The African Outlet* (524 Octavia Street), a tiny shop packed impossibly full with statues, masks, jewelry, rugs, clothing, ceremonial objects, and just about anything else made on the vast continent. From the instant you push your way through the beads at the entrance, thousands of items compete for your attention, with one stacked upon another in such a way that more than two patrons in the shop at one time makes for complete gridlock. Nigerian owner Horgan Edet has run this shop for many years, more than a decade in the present location, using a network of friends around Africa to find and buy his items. He's generally on hand and is happy to spend a few minutes explaining the provenance of a given item or holding forth on the strengths and weaknesses of the 49ers. Space may be at a premium, but

Edet finds room for a television on football Sundays. Open daily from 10:30 A.M. to 7:00 P.M. Call 864–3576.

Fancy eateries have sprung up all over Hayes Valley in the last fifteen years. One of the hippest spots on hip Hayes Street is **Frjtz** (579 Hayes Street), pronounced *freets*, a restaurant centered around the Belgian obsession with french fries. Although America has given the French credit for the beloved crispy, golden potatoes, the Belgians actually invented them, or at least raised them to an art form. Frjtz dishes them out the way they do on the streets of Brussels, soaking through a cone of white paper, with plenty of mayonnaise for dipping. For those who find the white stuff unsuitable as a condiment, there are other sauces to choose from, including curry and ketchup with a spicy kick, strawberry mustard, and a chipotle remoulade. A cone of fries and a strong Belgian beer make for the perfect afternoon or late-night snack, but sandwiches and crepes are on the menu to make it a meal. The hipster vibe comes from the art and photography exhibits that line the walls, and the pair of turntables wedged in next to the cash register. DJs spin electronica and house music on Friday night and Sunday afternoon, drawing in the neighborhood's cool set. The music can get loud enough to drown out anything below a shout, but a patio in back provides a somewhat calmer setting. Open Monday through Thursday 9:00 A.M. to 10:00 P.M., Friday until midnight, Saturday 10:00 A.M. to midnight, and Sunday 10:00 A.M. to 9:00 P.M. Call 864–7654 or visit www.frjtzfries.com. Hip and successful, Frjtz opened a second venue in Ghirardelli Square. Inexpensive.

For the art-cafe experience in a less frenetic environment, make a left on Laguna Street and head for **Momi Toby's Revolution Cafe** (528 Laguna Street). A strongly local contingent haunts this place, reading, writing, or chatting for hours on end. Many come in just for coffee, but tasty sandwiches, hearty soups, and pastries are also served. The owners restored the century-old bakery building, leaving such features as the separate rooms for toilet and sink that give it an old-world vibe. Despite the name, the cafe is not necessarily a place to plot the overthrow of the government. The name comes from the owner's great-grandmother, who cooked for Pancho Villa during the Mexican Revolution. The

movieset

The building at the northeast corner of Hayes and Laguna Streets, now an Indian restaurant, was used in 1923 as a location for the movie *Greed,* set in Gold Rush–era San Francisco. The director, Erich von Stroheim, found the Victorian building perfect for housing the fictional dentist's office of the main character. Stroheim, a known perfectionist, had a sign erected advertising the dentist's office; it was real enough to draw people with toothaches in off the street.

art covering the walls is local, some of it extremely so, formerly made at a print shop downstairs called Tinhorn Press. **_Tinhorn Press_** (511 Laguna Street) is now a full-fledged gallery across the street, owned by artist Terry Chastain and master printer John Gruenwald, who started Momi Toby's. Call 621–1292 or visit www.tinhorngallery.com. From time to time, the cafe hosts live music and poetry readings. Open Monday through Friday 7:30 A.M. to 10:00 P.M., Saturday and Sunday 8:00 A.M. to 10:00 P.M. Call 626–1508. Inexpensive.

Plenty of Hayes Valley demonstrates the way a downtrodden area can recover, but the **_Tenderloin_** to the north and east of the Civic Center complex is not gentrified. This is the traditional red-light district—rare and raunchy at night—named for a prime cut of beef once bought by policemen whose hard-duty pay for patrolling the district afforded the best. This area, wedged tightly between the seat of government and the well-to-do areas of Nob Hill and Union Square, is home to many of the city's single-room-occupancy hotels, and the streets are marked by drug-dealing, prostitution, and the mentally ill home-less. Yet two decades of immigration from Vietnam are changing some of the character, and notably the food, available in the Tenderloin. In February 2004, San Francisco designated two blocks of Larkin Street (from Eddy Street to O'Farrell Street) as "Sai Gon Nho," Little Saigon. Green and yellow banners emblazoned with a turn-of-the-twentieth-century French market as it presum-ably looked in the original Saigon, mark the streets of Little Saigon. At the por-tals of Little Saigon, poolside at the Phoenix Hotel, is **_Bambuddha Lounge_** (601 Eddy Street). Seductive Asian decor, complete with a reclining Buddha on the roof, and inside Buddha heads, full-size Buddha statues, and Southeast Asian art set up a nostalgic, retro feel. As down and out as the Tenderloin is in the streets, it's the opposite at this hip restaurant and bar. Waterfalls, a stand of live bam-boo, dark wood, low, cushioned daybeds by the hotel pool, and soft lighting are romantic, verging on overwhelming. The menu borrows from Burma, Thailand, Laos, Malaysia, Vietnam, and Java. The Lychee-tini (gin, Cointreau, lychee juice, and its fruit), one of many exotically named drinks, is best imbibed at the lively circular bar beyond the wall-to-ceiling waterfall. After 9:00 P.M., DJs spin music for a pop scene that includes models and trendy want-to-be-seens. Open Tues-day to Wednesday 5:00 to 11:00 P.M., Thursday and Friday to 2:00 A.M., and Sat-urday 6:00 P.M. to 2:00 A.M. Call 885–5086 or visit www.bambuddhalounge.com.

Early each year, Tet, the Vietnamese Lunar New Year, draws thousands to the Tenderloin to watch lions and dragons dance, taste Vietnamese snacks, and touch base with the 250 Vietnamese-owned businesses and 2,000 Vietnamese-American residents of the neighborhood. The Tenderloin is mostly safe during daylight hours. Women should be very careful in this part of town at night, however, and should travel with a companion.

The spiritual heart of the Tenderloin, and the place that makes it livable for many of the area's poorest people, is *Glide Memorial Church* (330 Ellis Street). If you happen to be in town on a weekend, do yourself a favor and get to one of the two Sunday "celebrations." Whether you are religious or not, chances are you will be moved. The 140-person all-volunteer Glide Ensemble choir rattles the roof with a booming mix of gospel, jazz, and a certain rock-and-roll energy that gets people out of their seats. Perhaps the most diverse crowd to be found anywhere in the city turns up to hear the choir and the powerful sermons by the Reverend Cecil Williams. Doctors and lawyers in suits and ties listen and nod their heads along with people who not too long ago might have been living on the streets. Glide's importance to the Tenderloin goes well beyond the joy and fun of the celebrations. The church also runs a free health clinic, builds housing for the homeless, helps with legal problems and employment counseling, and serves up one million meals a year to San Francisco's hungriest. Services Sunday at 9:00 and 11:00 A.M. Call 674–6000 or visit www.glide.org. Muni Bus 27, Muni Metro to Powell.

Despite the forbidding atmosphere, or perhaps because of it, the Tenderloin is home to some of the city's most interesting nightspots. Since 1972 *The Great American Music Hall* (859 O'Farrell Street) has been a top venue for local and national acts and provides a very intimate setting. It might be worth buying a ticket even if you're not a fan of the evening's band, just to get a look at the interior decor. This is a music hall in the old style, with ornately carved balconies around three sides held up by marble columns, and frescoes on the high ceilings. Today, despite its location next to San Francisco's most famous strip joint, the Great American strictly hosts legitimate musical acts, serving light food, full dinners, and bar beverages. Its past, however, is much less savory and much more interesting. Opened just after the 1906 earthquake, it was home to Blanco's, one of the city's more popular bordellos up until its closing in 1933.

Three years later it reopened as a dance club called the Music Box. The new club was owned by Sally Rand, a dancer and businesswoman who had come to fame and a small fortune after performing at the Chicago Century of Progress Exposition in 1933. Her dances at the world's fair got her arrested for obscenity, and soon she was famous and earning $6,000 a week dancing during the Great Depression. Rand came to San Francisco in 1939 for the Treasure Island World's Fair, where she set up one of its most popular attractions: the Sally Rand Nude Ranch, featuring women dancing in nothing but boots, gun belts, and cowboy hats. The highlight of an evening at the Music Box was said to be her risqué "fan dance," but few details are available. Check the newspaper, visit www.musichallsf.com, or call 885–0750 for information about upcoming concerts. Muni Bus 38.

The perfect spot to go before a show at the Great American, or for just about any other occasion, is *Edinburgh Castle* (950 Geary Street). It's a bit grungy, sure, and the lighting isn't great, but the Castle's charm is infectious. The bar is well stocked with beers from the British Isles and Scotland in particular and, of course, a wide selection of single-malt scotches. On either side above the main bar area are balconies with couches and tables ideal for more intimate conversations. If you get hungry before 11:00 P.M., your server will happily run around the corner to fetch you some fish and chips—wrapped in newspaper, naturally—from the shop owned by the same people. The Castle also hosts a number of cultural events: everything from rock bands and stand-up comics to theater productions and literary readings by any Scottish author who happens to be in town. The highlight of the year is Burns Night, January 25, a celebration of the birthday of the great Scottish poet Robert Burns. It seems every Scot in the city turns out to drink heavily, read poems, listen to bagpipes, and stab the haggis. Open daily from 5:00 P.M. to 2:00 A.M. Call 885–4074 or visit www.castlenews.com. Muni Bus 38.

Places to Stay near the Civic Center

Albion House Inn
135 Gough Street
621–0896
www.albionhouseinn.com
Cozy, quiet, and built of redwood in 1907, this restored nine-room Edwardian inn covers its walls with large paintings by Russian artist Sachal. Wine and cheese is served by the parlor fireplace. Moderate.

Hayes Valley Inn
417 Gough Street
431–9131
www.hayesvalleyinn.com
Providing clean, simple rooms with bathrooms down the hall in the heart of fun Hayes Valley, this inn advertises itself as gay friendly and pet friendly. With a common kitchen that anyone can use, this is about as relaxed as a hotel gets. Inexpensive.

Inn at the Opera
333 Fulton Street
863–8400
www.innattheopera.com
A small hotel that combines luxury with coziness, Inn at the Opera is one of the city's finest hotels. Its location a half block from the Opera House makes it a natural for visiting musicians, or those in town for the opera, ballet, or symphony. Expensive.

Phoenix Hotel
601 Eddy Street
776–1380
www.jduhospitality.com/hotels/hotel/12
This Tenderloin hotel's 1950s Hollywood vibe has a reputation for catering to actors and rock stars. As an added benefit, downstairs is Bambuddha Lounge. Stay here if you value personality in hotels. Inexpensive.

Places to Eat near the Civic Center

Absinthe
398 Hayes Street
551–1590
www.absinthe.com
This very popular, very stylish brasserie restaurant serves French-Californian cuisine. The bartenders take pride in mixing exotic drinks, but, alas, not the one the place is named for. Open Tuesday through Friday 11:30 to 2:00 A.M., Saturday 10:30 to 2:00 A.M., Sunday 10:30 A.M. to midnight. Moderate.

Arlequin

384B Hayes Street

626–1211

Owned by the same people who run Absinthe, Arlequin serves French comfort foods to go or to eat at the counter in the window. After enjoying French onion soup or a croque monsieur, be sure to save room for one of the house-made cakes and pastries. Open Monday through Friday 8:00 A.M. to 7:00 P.M., Saturday 9:00 A.M. to 8:00 P.M., Sunday noon to 6:00 P.M. Inexpensve.

Espetus

1686 Market Street

552–8792

www.espetus.com

A hankering for meat, Brazilian style, impels patrons of this *churrascaria* to eat their fill by letting weaving waiters in black with red scarves deftly carve beef, chicken, lamb, or pork from long skewers. Self-serve salad fills out the meal, unless you can't resist papaya cream with cassis for dessert. Open Monday through Saturday 11:30 A.M. to 3:30 P.M., Monday through Thursday 5:00 P.M. to 10:00 P.M., Friday and Saturday to 10:30 P.M. Moderate.

Hayes Street Grill

320 Hayes Street

863–5545

www.hayesstreetgrill.com

A classic, old-style restaurant, Hayes Street Grill serves some of the best seafood in town. With no-nonsense decor and a straight-ahead menu, this place has no interest in being trendy. Owner Patricia Unterman, former *Chronicle* food critic, knows what her customers want and gives it to them. Open Monday through Friday 10:30 A.M. to 9:30 P.M., Saturday 4:00 to 10:00 P.M., Sunday 4:00 to 8:00 P.M. Moderate.

Max's Opera Cafe

601 Van Ness Avenue

771–7301

This deli down the street from the Opera House specializes in enormous New York–style deli sandwiches, like pastrami and corned beef, named after prominent locals. Expect a raucous atmosphere and waiters who are given to singing. Open Sunday through Tuesday 11:30 A.M. to 10:00 P.M., Wednesday and Thursday until 11:00 P.M., Friday and Saturday until 11:30 P.M. Inexpensive.

Suppenküche

601 Hayes Street

252-9289

www.suppenkuche.com

Pining for Bavarian homestyle cooking? Kartoffelsuppe (potato soup), potato pancakes, cheese spätzle, pork loin, venison, and meatloaf will sate hearty appetites. Open daily 5:00 to 10:00 P.M. and Sunday 10:00 A.M. to 2:30 P.M. Moderate.

Vicolo Pizzeria

201 Ivy Street

863–2382

The name is Italian for *alley,* and that's where it is, on a small street behind Davies Symphony Hall. The specialty is gourmet pizzas, with three kinds of mushrooms or four kinds of cheese. What makes it irresistible, though, is the fluffy cornmeal crust. This is a great spot for a presymphony bite, and you are likely to see people carrying instruments in and out. Open Sunday through Thursday 5:00 to 8:00 P.M., Friday and Saturday to 9:00 P.M. Inexpensive.

Zuni Cafe

1658 Market Street

552–2522

Set in a triangular building with windows all around, Zuni exudes cool. Relax at the long bar and slurp down one of the many varieties of oysters on the menu, or choose a table and peruse the fine Mediterranean menu. Sit downstairs in the area behind the bar, if you can. Open Tuesday through Saturday 11:30 A.M. to midnight, Sunday 11:00 A.M. to 11:00 P.M. Moderate.

Downtown

Like everything else in San Francisco, the word *downtown* can mean many things. The most obvious and most universally accepted definition is the **Financial District,** the patch of high-rise office buildings clustered around the eastern end of Market Street. Despite the name, the Financial District is not the soulless region of metal, glass, and empty suits that you might imagine. Those things are there, San Francisco being a capital of West Coast banking and finance, but the Financial District and the rest of Downtown also present the most vivid reminders of old-time San Francisco. From the banks that grew wealthy on gold money, to the streets designed for cable cars and trolleys, there is a lot of history in the skyscraper canyons, if you know where to look.

The logical place to begin a tour of downtown San Francisco is at the **Ferry Building** (Market Street at The Embarcadero), whose clock tower has beckoned to those arriving in the city by boat since 1898. Many commuters and shoppers from towns along the bay still choose to come to San Francisco by ferry rather than fight the maddening traffic, but the port's heyday was in its early days, before the Golden Gate and Bay Bridges made arrival by car possible. San Francisco's location at the end of a peninsula has its benefits, but before the bridges

DOWNTOWN

Amtrak Depot
STEUART ST
DAVIS ST
BATTERY ST
SANSOME ST
FINANCIAL DISTRICT
MONTGOMERY ST
MARKET ST
COMMERCIAL ST
KEARNY ST
COLUMBUS AVE
CHINATOWN
Portsmouth Square
Old St. Mary's Cathedral
GRANT AVE
STOCKTON ST
MAIDEN LN
MARK LN
Union Square
GEARY ST
BURRITT ST
POWELL ST
ELLIS ST
Cable Car Barn
MASON ST
Huntington Park
NOB HILL
TAYLOR ST
Grace Cathedral
JONES ST
LEAVENWORTH
CLAY ST
SACRAMENTO ST
HYDE ST
PACIFIC AVE
JACKSON ST
WASHINGTON ST
LARKIN ST
CALIFORNIA ST
PINE ST
BUSH ST
SUTTER ST
POST ST
POLK ST
VAN NESS AVE
101

.25 mi
.25 km
0
0
N

were built in the late 1930s, it left the city somewhat isolated. This problem was pointed out most clearly in the construction of the transcontinental railroad, completed in 1869. Even though the men who financed the project all lived in San Francisco, they chose Oakland, across the bay, as the western terminus, rather than run track south along the bay and back up the peninsula. This meant that all passengers traveling to San Francisco from points east had to get off the train in Oakland and board a boat for San Francisco. At its peak in the 1920s and 1930s, the Ferry Building was the busiest transit hub in the nation, with some 50 million passengers crossing its lobby each year. Before the advent of the skyscraper, the Ferry Building's 245-foot tower, modeled after the Giralda Tower in Seville, Spain, made it the tallest building in the city.

Years of neglect left the building nearly obsolete and close to decrepit. A renovated Ferry Building opened in 2003 with a 660-foot-long, skylight-topped nave. In the center of the 22,000-square-foot mosaic tile floor below is the Great Seal of the State of California, a reproduction of the original that had been on that spot. Along each side of the Ferry Building's Ground Floor Marketplace, arranged in the style of a European food hall, are forty food, wine, and produce outlets representing the most famous of the San Francisco Bay Area's artisan comestible producers. Taste cheese and handcrafted breads, or pop into a name restaurant like the Slanted Door to dine on delicate Vietnamese dishes. In good weather, exit with picnic provisions on the east side of the building towards the ferry piers. Bayside Plaza has free views of Treasure Island and the San Francisco–Oakland Bay Bridge.

three-dotway

Herb Caen raised newspaper column writing to an art, a form of shorthand journalism that garnered a Pulitzer Prize. For fifty-seven years, the hat-wearing, pigeon-hating, man-about-town chronicler sifted through gossip items, celebrity sightings, births, and deaths, with occasional trips to his personal mecca, Paris. It was high-level doggerel, or for holidays like New Year's Day, a rhyming prose poem of dropped names, each item separated with three dots. On July 14, 1996, when Caen was eighty, San Francisco named a 3.2-mile stretch of The Embarcadero from China Basin to Fisherman's Wharf, Herb Caen Way . . . (three dots included).

The *Ferry Plaza Farmers Market* (291–3276, www.ferryplazafarmers market.com) operates four days a week, year-round, or as the publicity says, "rain or shine." Farmers and artisan producers, many from California's Central Valley, spread out from the Ferry Building arcades onto the Embarcadero Plaza. The organic and sustainable produce market on Saturday schedules free "Shop with the Chef" tours and food preparation demonstrations. In good weather the

Saturday Market becomes a social meeting place for up to 15,000 shoppers, dog-walkers, parents with strollers, noshers, and people watchers. Fruits, vegetables, flowers, meats, fish, breads, and cheese are featured on Saturday, Tuesday, and Thursday. Sunday's Garden Market shows off the best from Northern California nurseries.

Walking west from the Ferry Building across *The Embarcadero*, with Muni F Line historic streetcars rolling by, it is hard to believe that for several decades this broad boulevard was covered by a hideous elevated freeway. As with the Central Freeway above the Hayes Valley neighborhood, the Embarcadero Freeway loomed menacingly over the street, providing limitless opportunities for crime, and making the journey to and from the Ferry an unpleasant experience. Like the Central, the Embarcadero Freeway was deemed unsafe after the 1989 earthquake, and its demolition in 1992 was met with great rejoicing. Since then, city leaders have made a point of refurbishing the Embarcadero area, and the results are wonderful.

Once Feared, Now Honored

Immediately across from the Ferry Building is *Harry Bridges Plaza,* an unlikely tribute to a man who was widely hated by the powerful in San Francisco during his day. Bridges, born in Melbourne, Australia, in 1901, joined the Merchant Marines at age sixteen, and in 1922 made his way to San Francisco where he became a longshoreman. Appalled at working conditions of his colleagues, who came to the docks each day not knowing if they would have a job and often had to bribe the foreman to get work, he began agitating, and formed a union among longshoremen and all other marine laborers. On May 9, 1934, with the nation deep in the Great Depression, his Joint Marine Strike Committee called a general strike and shut down the city's shipping industry. On July 3, a day that would be called "Bloody Thursday," business interests tried to break the strike, and a pitched battle ensued between union members and police, mostly in the Rincon Hill neighborhood. "Police used their clubs freely and mounted officers rode into milling crowds," the *San Francisco News* reported. "The strikers fought back using fists, boards and bricks as weapons." The strike was eventually settled, with the intervention of President Franklin D. Roosevelt, and Bridges continued to grow in stature. Despite efforts in the 1950s to paint Bridges as a communist—and despite an overturned perjury charge for saying he was not a communist—he became indispensable, to the point where the mayor named him to the port's board of directors.

The plaza, at Market and Steuart Streets, itself is just an expanse of concrete in the middle of The Embarcadero, around which the F-Line streetcars turn. Aside from being a main gathering point for San Francisco's New Year's Eve festivities, not much actually goes on in the plaza. Still, it is much nicer than the freeway that used to cover it.

Where Geary and Kearny Streets both pour into Market Street, a monument stands, painted gold with a lamp at the top. This is ***Lotta's Fountain,*** named for Lotta Crabtree, a nationally famous actress who got her start at age six, singing and dancing for miners in the Gold Country. In 1850 Lotta's parents moved the family from New York to Grass Valley, California, where she became a protégé of famed actress Lola Montez. Lotta began touring the taverns where miners congregated, her mother gratefully collecting the bags of gold nuggets thrown onstage. The family moved to San Francisco, and Lotta became a hit in the big city's theaters, earning the moniker "Miss Lotta, San Francisco Favorite." She soon began touring nationally, became a huge star, and retired at age forty-five. Lotta came out of retirement at age sixty-eight for one last public performance, at San Francisco's Panama Pacific International Exposition in 1915.

Lotta commissioned the fountain, a simple bronze tower with a lamp at the top, in 1875, having it cast in Philadelphia and shipped around the tip of South America. The workmanship turned out to be excellent, as it survived the 1906 earthquake and became a symbol for San Francisco's resilience. It is the traditional site for the earthquake memorial, held at 5:13 A.M. on April 18. Today, water flows from the fountain only on that day and on September 9, the day of California's admission to the Union. The fountain's most famous moment came on Christmas Eve 1910, when Luisa Tetrazzini, the greatest opera diva of her day, sang in front of it as throngs packed Market Street. The soprano had been embroiled in a court battle over a contract to sing in New York, saying that her manager had booked her to perform in San Francisco at the same time. "I will sing in San Francisco if I have to sing there in the streets, for I know the streets of San Francisco are free," she told reporters, and she made good on her promise.

Once the Gold Rush got going, not only were there suddenly a lot more people in San Francisco, there were a lot more people with a lot more money in their pockets. Besides the newly flush miners and the merchants and tradespeople who catered to them, the streets were full of ne'er-do-wells anxious to get their hands on some of the loot. So smart entrepreneurs soon opened banks, to help secure fortunes. These companies are among the earliest surviving from the city's history, and a few of them have set up exhibits to tell their tales.

The ***Wells Fargo History Museum*** (420 Montgomery Street) is devoted mostly to the stagecoach system that the bank operated to move people to and from the gold mines throughout the West, and to bring newcomers to the region from the Mississippi River, in those days the western terminus of the railroad. Besides the human cargo, Wells Fargo stagecoaches were also the

Wells Fargo stagecoach

standard way to ship precious metals. At points during the mining booms, Wells Fargo stages were moving more than two-thirds of the gold and silver that the west was producing. Because so much of the shiny stuff passed through Wells Fargo's hands, the federal government took to using the Wells Fargo ledgers as quasi-official statistics on western production of precious metals.

The museum's bottom floor has a number of interesting artifacts from those days, including displays of the different types and qualities of gold found in mines and rivers throughout the Gold Country. A little more than a pinch of gold from each of sixty different veins is displayed—behind glass, in case you get any ideas—ranging from dark brown powder to brilliant gold flakes. Have a look also at the relief maps of the country and the region, to get a picture of just how long and how tricky some of the journeys must have been.

The best part of the museum is on the top floor, where you can squeeze into an actual stagecoach and imagine a trip through the Sierra Nevada. The padded seats might feel reasonably comfortable at first, until you realize nine people would have been crammed onto the three tiny benches, and you could have sat in this one spot for as long as a month. If you thought your last car ride with the family to Aunt Betty's was a trial, listen to one passenger's description of his trip: "A through-ticket and 15 inches of seat, with a fat man on one side, a poor widow on the other, a baby in your lap, a bandbox over your head, and three or more persons immediately in front, leaning against your knees, making the picture, as well as the sleeping place, for the trip."

Stops along the way were hardly luxurious either. Food on the month-long trip from St. Louis to San Francisco consisted mostly of boiled black beans and coffee, passengers sometimes were told to get out and walk alongside the carriage during tricky parts of the trail, and chances to wash oneself were few and far between. Another passenger describes how by the end of the trip the passengers were coated in a black film of grime. How they must have smelled is too frightening to think about. Open Monday through Friday 9:00 A.M. to 5:00 P.M. Admission is free. Call 396–2619 or visit www.wellsfargohistory.com/muse ums/sfmuseum.html.

Around the corner from the Wells Fargo Museum, in the classically austere Bank of California building, is the **Bank of California Museum** (400 California Street). As the name implies, it shows the various currency systems used during the Gold Rush. In many cases, miners simply carried around pouches of gold flakes and dust. In order to conduct commerce, merchants either had to weigh the gold themselves, or estimate the amount to charge: a pinch of dust for a pint of ale, for example. With so much gold floating around, a system was needed to regulate its use. The United States government didn't open a mint in town until 1854, by which time many banks had already sprung up to press their own coinage. Additionally, many forms of foreign currency were in use, some of which were imported to make up for the lack of small change in the economy. The twelve-and-a-half-cent Spanish *real* was widely used and was referred to as a "bit," leading to the once common practice of calling a quarter "two bits." Many of these early coins are on display in the museum's cases, along with the instruments used to measure them. Because the coins were made of solid gold, unscrupulous sorts may have been tempted to shave a bit off before passing them along. For this reason, banks used plierlike tools

Something for Everyone

One thing that makes the Financial District more pleasant than the average office district is a city requirement that all high-rise buildings include space that is open to the general public. Thus many have wide-open lobbies that provide a pleasant way to walk from one street to another, courtyards to eat lunch in, public art projects, or roof gardens with excellent views.

One of the nicest is the **Southern Pacific Building** (One Market Street), former headquarters of the famous railroad. On the seventh floor is a roof garden, mostly used by office workers on their lunch and cigarette breaks, with views out over the bay toward Oakland. This building's view was critical to the railroad company's success in its early days, as employees could spot the ferries as they came in from Oakland, the terminus of the transcontinental railroad. Thus they knew exactly when the valuable cargo from the east would reach the peninsula. Now it just provides a nice vantage point on the city.

Just about any high-rise you walk into in the financial district will have some public space. Ask the security guards how to get there.

TOP ATTRACTIONS DOWNTOWN

The Embarcadero	Xanadu Gallery/Folk Art International
Lotta's Fountain	Grace Cathedral
Bank of California Museum	Cable Car Barn
Portsmouth Square	

with round slots the exact diameter of each denomination of coin to verify that the currency hadn't been tampered with.

The **Bank of California** (400 California Street), now called Union Bank of California, was founded in 1864 by William Chapman Ralston, who through it helped to shape San Francisco. Ralston invested heavily in Nevada silver mines and amassed enough capital to invest in just about everything under the sun. Included in these varied endeavors were importing silkworms from China, an attempt to grow Cuban tobacco in California's San Joaquin Valley, bankrolling the exploration of Alaska, building the Palace Hotel, and breeding racehorses. His love for the equestrian arts was well known to the people of the area, as he could sometimes be seen on horseback, racing the trains that chugged up the peninsula. Ralston took the Bank of California's affairs personally—a little too personally, it turned out. In 1875 when the silver mines dried up and a general financial panic caused a run on banks, it was discovered that Ralston, heavily in debt, had been tapping the bank's reserve for his personal use. The day the bank's money ran out and the board asked for Ralston's resignation, he took his daily swim in the bay and never returned, presumably having drowned. Call 291–4653. Open Monday through Friday 9:00 A.M. to 5:00 P.M. Admission is free.

One block down from the Wells Fargo Museum is **First Bank** (550 Montgomery Street), site of a more recent bit of banking history. Starting in 1906, just three months after the Great Earthquake, this was the headquarters of the Bank of Italy. A. P. Giannini, founder of the bank, later changed its name to Bank of America and first developed the idea of branch banking. The building is a National Historic Landmark, partly because of its place in the history of American banking, but also because of its gorgeous interior, with original marble floors and carved ceilings. Open Monday through Thursday 9:00 A.M. to 4:00 P.M., and Friday 9:00 A.M. to 5:00 P.M. Visit www.firstbanks.com/about/550 MontgomerySt.asp.

Across Montgomery Street, where it meets the alley of Merchant Street, is a plaque marking the ***Western Terminus of the Pony Express.*** By 1860, San Francisco was a city of considerable wealth, with an established business community longing for contact with their peers in the east. The stagecoaches worked well and were a much faster conveyance than the steamships sailing down to Panama, but it still took twenty days to get a message to St. Joseph, Missouri, the westernmost point of the railroad and the telegraph. This seemed particularly long when it came to the delivery of mail, and a new system was sought to transmit messages. Three businessmen developed the new service, buying 600 of the fastest horses they could find and hiring seventy-five riders, each of whom had to weigh less than 110 pounds and be able to defend himself from attacks by Indians. Advertisements for riders stated, "orphans preferred," showing how confident the owners were that the horsemen would make it back safely.

The men rode day and night, each one traveling 60 miles at top speed, on a new horse every 10 miles, before handing the packet off to the next man. Once the mail reached Sacramento, it was loaded onto a boat and sent to San Francisco. Delivery time was cut to ten days, and the new service was a hit. The success was destined to be short-lived, though, as technological progress moved inexorably west. By early 1862, the telegraph wire reached California, and the Pony Express went out of business, having lasted only two years but living on in the legend of the West.

While walking up Commercial Street, stop for a moment at ***Empire Park*** (between Montgomery and Kearny Streets), a monument to San Francisco's all-time greatest eccentric. Considering the collection of characters that have always gravitated here, this is quite an accomplishment, but Emperor Norton was nothing if not ambitious. A wealthy merchant, he tried to corner the West Coast rice market only to fail and be left penniless. He didn't let being broke spoil his visions of grandeur, however, and declared himself emperor of the United States and king of Mexico. He strutted around town in regal fashion, eventually becoming a celebrity. Restaurateurs, well aware that he was broke, invited him in and treated him to a meal because he always drew a crowd of well-wishers. He eventually even printed currency from his mythical empire. The park, built on the spot where Norton lived, has a few tables and benches ideal for munching a bag lunch.

Right next to the Financial District is ***Chinatown***, where some of the city's most interesting blocks still teem with Chinese immigrants both old and new. Chinese were among the first people to arrive in San Francisco, and they were discriminated against from the start. Indeed, one of the reasons Chinatown is so self-contained and it is so easy to tell when you have left its confines is that

A Dash of History

Most of the time you see a plaque marking a historical event in San Francisco, you can trust that the event in question actually took place. Not so with a marking on the obscure alley of Burritt Street, which ducks briefly off Bush Street above the Stockton Tunnel. The plaque matter-of-factly states:

ON APPROXIMATELY THIS SPOT MILES ARCHER, PARTNER OF SAM SPADE, WAS DONE IN BY BRIGID O'SHAUGHNESSY.

You might feel bad for poor Miles, even if Sam didn't. He never really liked Miles, and showed it by sleeping with his wife. As for the treacherous Miss O'Shaughnessy, the last we saw of her was in an elevator, headed down for a long stint behind bars courtesy of Sam's tip-off to the cops.

The names in question are, of course, characters in Dashiell Hammett's classic San Francisco novel *The Maltese Falcon.* If you haven't read it—or seen the movie with Humphrey Bogart—I've just ruined the ending, but get yourself to a bookstore anyway. Hammett, a former Pinkerton detective, lived and wrote in San Francisco and made the city a central location in his stories. His exacting way of writing is what makes plaques like this one possible. The book is peppered with references to specific street corners, restaurants, and streetcar lines, making it an indispensable companion for a visitor to the city.

For more of the Hammett experience, take Don Herron's walking tour to all of the places haunted by Spade, the Continental Op, and Dash himself. Check www.donherron.com/tour.html for times and locations.

If you can't make the tour, at least stop in *John's Grill* (63 Ellis Street; www .johnsgrill.com), where Sam Spade liked to sup on chops, baked potatoes, and sliced tomatoes. You too can enjoy this tasty meal, while checking out a vast collection of *Maltese Falcon* memorabilia.

in the early days it was essentially a Chinese ghetto. All Chinese who came to California were required to live there, and it is still today the most densely populated area of the city. In the nineteenth century, Chinese people outside of the neighborhood could be stopped by police and given a quiz to make sure they were Chinatown residents. For this reason, many Chinese people who lived and worked elsewhere carried cheat sheets with Chinese characters that gave the answers to the questions.

Chinatown's nucleus is **Portsmouth Square** (Kearny Street between Clay and Washington Streets), where you will usually find gaggles of elderly Chinese men playing cards and Chinese chess and hanging out. The square was once the center of action for the whole city, not just for Chinatown. It is named after the ship captained by John B. Montgomery, which sailed into San Francisco in 1846 to claim the land for the United States. Montgomery planted the Stars and Stripes in this square, and a flagpole installed in 1924 marks the spot today. The square also has a memorial to the author Robert Louis Stevenson, who lived in San Francisco for six months during 1879–1880. He was hanging out waiting for the woman he loved to get divorced and spent many of his idle hours writing in this square. The author of *Treasure Island* is honored with a bronze ship on a granite base.

Most of the tourist traffic is centered on Grant Avenue, but to experience the real Chinatown, walk another block west to **Stockton Street.** In the afternoons you will have to fight your way along the sidewalks as they become absurdly full of people doing their daily shopping at the countless groceries that line the street.

After you're done shopping, double back to Grant Avenue and work your way south to California Street. Here you'll find **Old Saint Mary's** (660 California Street), the state's first Catholic cathedral. The brick church opened on Christmas 1854, just weeks after the Pope declared the dogma of the Immaculate Conception of Mary, and thus was dedicated to the mother of Christ. The building itself has a number of diverse influences. The first Archbishop of San Francisco, Joseph Alemany, dictated that the church be modeled after one in his native Spain. The granite in its foundation was brought in from China, and the brick for the walls was sailed around the tip of South America from New England. The structure you see today is mostly original. The interior was completely redone after the fire of 1906 gutted the building, and it was reinforced against seismic disruption in 2002.

The traditional heart of downtown San Francisco is **Union Square,** a one-block park rededicated in 2002, with wide-open spaces replacing homeless-sheltering landscaping. The square is surrounded by high-end department stores and the ritzy, century-old Westin St. Francis Hotel. The square, characterized by a small hill in the center, gets its name from the pro-union rallies that took place there just prior to the Civil War. In its center is the 1903 Dewey Monument, in honor of Admiral Dewey's victory in the Spanish-American War. The 98-foot tower is topped by a bronze figure of a nude woman, representing Victory, carrying a wreath and a trident. The model for Robert Aitken's sculpture was Alma de Bretteville, a strapping young lady from a poor local family. Her 6-foot-tall frame and stunning looks also caught the eye of Adolph Spreckels, scion of a wealthy family that owned sugar plantations in Hawaii. Having found the ultimate sugar daddy, Alma became one of San Francisco's great philanthropists, building and donating the Palace of the Legion of Honor museum.

Most of the department stores that ring the square are standard issue, but a few have their unique points. For the most fun and exciting shopping experience

Ink-Stained Twain

San Francisco's newspaper circulation wars between major dailies the *Chronicle* and the *Examiner* were legendary, as much a battle between style and editorial page stance than editorial quality. After years of legally operating with separate staffs while publishing on shared presses, the economic battle for survival as the paper of record was won by economics. The morning-published *Chronicle*, slightly more liberal, and by far the most popular, remains. The company founded by William Randolph Hearst paid a local family to take the *Examiner* off its hands. That veteran paper, a tabloid-size shadow of its former conservative self, is still published and also online at www.examiner.com by yet another publisher. In the nineteenth century, however, several dailies fought it out each day on Market Street.

One of the papers that faded away was the *Call,* which lives on in memory for having given a young man from Missouri named Samuel Clemens his start as a writer. Clemens wrote hundreds of articles for the *Call,* and, as can be seen in the following sample from August 23, 1864, he hardly specialized in straight reporting:

"In consequence of the warm, close atmosphere which smothered the city at two o'clock yesterday afternoon, everybody expected to be shaken out of their boots by an earthquake before night, but up to the hour of our going to press the supernatural bootjack had not arrived yet. That is just what makes it so unhealthy— the earthquakes are getting so irregular. When a community get [sic] used to a thing, they suffer when they have to go without it. However, the trouble cannot be remedied; we know of nothing that will answer as a substitute for one of those convulsions—to an unmarried man."

in the district, try the **Levi's Store** (300 Post Street). San Francisco being the home of Levi Strauss, the store naturally carries the full line of the company's apparel. Call 501–0100.

Ducking off Union Square's eastern edge, **Maiden Lane** is now a genteel alley of fancy shops and sidewalk cafes, but during Gold Rush days it was San Francisco's most notorious street of sin. This is saying something, because in those days prostitution ran rampant in the young city. Of the people pouring into San Francisco, maybe one in thirty was a woman, resulting in hordes of unaccompanied and badly behaved men. Entrepreneurs saw an opportunity, naturally, and they began importing young women to the city, often under false pretenses, to serve in the brothels. Historian Herbert Asbury, in his 1933 book *The Barbary Coast,* wrote that in 1850 alone some 2,000 prostitutes arrived in town, many of them seasoned veterans from New York, New Orleans, and European cities. Many of the women were Asian or Mexican, but the most valuable and expensive were the Europeans.

Red-light districts sprang up in Chinatown and all along the Barbary Coast, but the worst of them all was Morton Street, as Maiden Lane was then known. The alley was full of brothels known as "cribs," where the prostitutes were said to be the most open to depravity, and perhaps because of this were among the most popular. The girls were known to lean out the window and shout to the men passing by. Once the men went inside, the cribs often had secret entrances so that thieves in cahoots with the prostitutes could sneak in to pick the men's pockets. This was also not a place for an "upstanding" woman to walk, as denizens of the cribs would harangue them for "giving it away."

Prostitution still plagues other San Francisco districts, but by the turn of the twentieth century, the city managed to clean up Morton Street, renaming it Maiden Lane after a posh shopping street in London. Hidden in the alley is **Xanadu Gallery/Folk Art International** (140 Maiden Lane), the only non-residential building in San Francisco designed by architect Frank Lloyd Wright. The first striking thing about the building is its brick exterior, rare in San Francisco. Four concentric brick arches outline the doors, drawing you in even before your feet have turned to enter. After walking through a glass tunnel, you reach the interior, an igloo-shaped room with a ramp that spirals its way around the walls. Wright designed the building in 1948 for the V. C. Morris Gift Store, and the spiral ramp theme was one he would use again in New York's Guggenheim Museum.

Folk Art International, which bought and restored the building in 1979, is a gallery of mostly tribal art from around the world, including sculpture, totems, urns, boxes, and a nice collection of amber jewelry. As you spiral upward, admiring the pieces spaced along the built-in mahogany cabinets that Wright himself designed, remember one thing: Unless you are very lucky, this stuff is not going to look quite as good in your house. Open Monday through Saturday from 10:00 A.M. to 6:00 P.M.; closed Sunday. Call 392–9999.

Just west of Union Square is **Lefty O'Doul's** (333 Geary Street), a San Francisco institution with a long bar and a piano by the window for cheesy sing-alongs. A hofbrau where servers with big knives and paper hats will carve you a hot sandwich, the bar was established in 1958 by Lefty O'Doul, a San Francisco sports legend. San Francisco is a city very proud of its baseball history. Willie Mays, considered the best player ever by many professional baseball historians in the nation and every amateur historian here, played for the Giants. Willie's godson Barry Bonds, the single-season home run champ who surpassed his godfather's home run record in 2003, deposits baseballs into the bay all summer long. Before the Giants moved to town from New York, San Francisco's team was the Seals of the minor Pacific Coast League, the squad where local boy Joe DiMaggio got his start before the Yankees snatched him up. But O'Doul

AUTHORS' FAVORITES DOWNTOWN

Bank of California Museum	The Irish Bank
Portsmouth Square	Cable Car Barn

was San Francisco's first baseball hero: an all-hit, no-field outfielder for the New York Giants in the 1920s and 1930s who still holds the National League record for most hits in a season. The man who gave young DiMaggio his start as manager of the Seals from 1935 to 1951, O'Doul also had a reputation internationally. His organizing of American all-stars to travel to Japan made him a legend in that baseball-crazy country, and there is even a restaurant named for him in Vancouver, Canada, where he briefly managed a minor-league team. The walls of Lefty O'Doul's are covered with pictures and memorabilia of his career, but the best item up there is a blown-up copy of a USO ID card for one "Norma Jean DiMaggio." Open daily 7:00 to 2:00 A.M. Call 982–8900. Inexpensive.

Those who are hungry for a hearty breakfast and who, like many of us, can't resist a place that claims global renown in its name, should stop at *World Famous Sears Fine Food* (439 Powell Street). Founded in 1938 by Ben Sears—a retired circus clown—and his wife, Hilbur, the restaurant has changed hands a few times, moved a half block down Powell Street, and closed for renovations for part of 2003, but eating there still makes you feel like you're going back in time. This is the kind of place where the tablecloths are covered with sheets of plastic, where the deep pink of the waitresses' dresses matches the brushed pink wainscoting on the walls, and where you are guaranteed to be called "hon" several times. The signature dish, "Sears World Famous 18 Swedish Pancakes," is less daunting than it sounds, as each of the illustrious eighteen is about the size and thickness of a beer coaster. One tradition that, unfortunately, didn't last was the "Cadillac waiting room." In Sears's previous location, space was limited, and people often had to wait to sit down. There was nowhere to linger inside on the often cold mornings, however, so the owners parked a pair of pink Cadillacs outside with the heat and radio on, to make the waits more tolerable. Open daily 6:30 A.M. to 2:30 P.M. Call 986–1160. Inexpensive.

San Francisco's best Irish pub, *The Irish Bank* (10 Mark Lane), gained some notoriety shortly after its opening in 1996 when it clashed with an old-country institution. The pub, quickly a Financial District favorite, was originally called the Bank of Ireland, a moniker that didn't sit well with the real Bank of Ireland, where Dubliners keep their hard-earned euros. A nine-month legal battle ensued, and in 1997 the pub's owners agreed to alter the name enough to avoid confusion. Mayor Willie Brown presided over the name change on St. Patrick's Day, naturally. The pub is one of the more welcoming spots downtown, with an airy room perfect for a casual lunch, and, on a nice day, tables out in the private alley. For the most intimacy, however, grab the table for two that sits inside the wooden confessional booth. Lunch served daily, 11:30 A.M. to 3:00 P.M.; dinner served Monday through Saturday, 5:00 to 10:00 P.M., open for drinks until 2:00 A.M. Call 788–7152 or visit www.theirishbank.com. Inexpensive.

Take the California Street Cable Car line to get to **Nob Hill,** San Francisco's ritziest quarter, where the oldest of the old money lives. Today Nob Hill is dominated by a cathedral and luxury hotels, but it once was home to mansions of four men who were instrumental in the development of California, building vast fortunes in the process. Leland Stanford, Mark Hopkins, Collis Huntington, and Charles Crocker—known collectively as "The Big Four"—were successful merchants who sold hardware and groceries. With the aid of a ton of government money, they teamed up to oversee the construction of the transcontinental railroad. Each got extremely rich from the endeavor, and each soon built a spectacular home atop Nob Hill.

Nob Hill's centerpiece is the massive **Grace Cathedral** (1100 California Street), an Episcopal church built on the site where Charles Crocker's mansion stood before being razed by the 1906 earthquake. It is the third largest Episcopal cathedral in the country, behind St. John the Divine in New York and the National Cathedral in Washington, D.C. The massive stone structure holds a mishmash of objects from other places, including a fifteenth-century French limestone altar, an English gothic prayer desk, and doors made from the same mold as those on the Duomo in Florence. Also worth looking at are an icon of Martin Luther King Jr. and a sculpture of St. Francis of Assisi by local artist Beniamino Bufano.

Despite its affiliation with the Episcopal Church, Grace is really the cathedral of the city. Special occasions are often marked there, with the mayor, the board of supervisors, and other luminaries in attendance. One of Grace Cathedral's nicest features is the AIDS Interfaith Chapel, located just to the right of the main entrance. Intended as a place for all people to pray, the chapel is decorated with the symbols of ten different religions. The altarpiece is a metal triptych by artist Keith Haring, incorporating his signature rounded figures. Behind the altar hangs a piece of the AIDS quilt, which rotates every few months. Two labyrinths, one along the cathedral nave a la Chârtres, France, and one outside facing Huntington Park, draw meditators of all persuasions. Visit www.gracecathedral.org.

Across Taylor Street from Grace Cathedral is **Huntington Park,** where Collis Huntington's mansion once faced Crocker's before it met the same fate

Hallidie's Folly

The cable car was invented and developed by Andrew Hallidie, who (conveniently enough) owned a company that manufactured wire rope. He got the idea while standing on Nob Hill, watching a team of horses struggle to draw a carriage to the peak. The dirt roads were too slippery, and the horses began to slide back, eventually falling to their deaths. Appalled, and convinced that there had to be a better way to move people up and down the steep hills, he put his knowledge of rope to good use, opening the first line on September 1, 1873, along Clay Street between Van Ness Avenue and Kearny Street. The project was mocked at first, called "Hallidie's Folly," but it didn't take long to catch on. By 1880, nine different companies were running twenty-two separate cable car lines all over the city.

The number of lines dwindled over the years, and San Francisco, in a fit of modernization, nearly killed off its distinctive conveyance in 1947, when the board of supervisors announced plans to dismantle the system and replace it with electric buses. The public was outraged, but was thought to be powerless to stop the action. A local woman named Frieda Klussman disagreed and formed the Citizen's Committee to Save the Cable Cars. She successfully pushed for a public referendum on the matter, voters overwhelmingly rejected the bus plan, and Frieda became "The Woman Who Saved the Cable Cars."

in 1906. Huntington's widow donated the land to the city in 1915 to be turned into a public square. In the center is the Fountain of the Tortoises, a replica of one in Rome's Piazza Mattei. The playful fountain, showing children riding dolphins and, of course, tortoises climbing on top, once stood at Charles Crocker's mansion in Hillsborough, a town south of San Francisco.

Two blocks north on Mason Street, at the corner of Washington, is the **Cable Car Barn** (1201 Mason Street), part museum and part powerhouse for the system. Go straight downstairs first, and have a look at the large wheels or "sheaves" that spin continuously to move cable in and out. As you've walked around downtown, you have probably noticed a noise, a rumbling from under the earth when you get near the cable car tracks. Well, relax; these aren't small earthquakes. These are the cables, constantly moving whenever the system is running, just waiting for a car to hitch on and go for a ride.

A cable car has no engine, just a battery to run the lights. The cars are essentially conveyed up and down the hills in the same way you hold on to one of its handles. The gripman, who stands in the center of the car, pulls back on a handle to lower a steel vise, which grabs the cable running underground. This is called "taking rope," and he will try to do it gradually to avoid a sudden start. Whenever the car stops to take on or let off passengers, the gripman releases the vise and lets the cable fall. At certain points along the way, the cable is too low for the vise to grab, so the gripman uses a narrow hook, called a cable lifter, to pull it up into his grasp.

Upstairs, underneath the walkway, you will see four pairs of sheaves spinning cables around them in a figure eight pattern. Before you are also the four engines, each of which powers one line of cable. But wait, you say, having studied the map and read the introduction to this book. There are only three cable car lines. Why are there four engines? Well, there are three routes, but four lines of cable. The California Street line is simple, one line of cable running in a straight line. The other two routes are more complicated, however, both running up Powell Street before splitting off on their way to the wharf. So a single cable carries both lines' cars up Powell to the Cable Car Barn, where they switch to the Hyde Street cable and the Mason Street cable. Beyond the engines, in the back of the room, are four more sheaves, one for each line, which are mounted on carriages. These are the "tension sheaves," which slide along tracks to keep the cables taught as they stretch.

The cable car system is now a National Historic Landmark—the only one that moves. The Cable Car Barn is open April through September from 10:00 A.M. to 6:00 P.M., and October through March from 10:00 A.M. to 5:00 P.M. Admission is free. Call 474–1887 or visit www.cablecarmuseum.com.

Places to Stay Downtown

Hotel Astoria
510 Bush Street
434–8889
This comfortable budget hotel is very well located near Chinatown, Nob Hill, and Union Square. The rooms aren't exciting, but they are clean and relatively quiet. Bathrooms are down the hall. Inexpensive.

Hotel Huntington
1075 California Street
474–5400
www.huntingtonhotel.com
One of several fine luxury hotels at the loftiest height of Nob Hill, this towering building is on the spot where Collis Huntington's mansion stood before it burned in 1906. The rooms combine antique furniture with modern appointments, including Internet connections. Don't miss the ground-floor restaurant, The Big 4, which contains a wealth of railroad memorabilia. Expensive.

Hotel Triton
342 Grant Street
394–0500
www.hoteltriton.com
This may be the rarest hotel of all: It provides the finest of everything plus a sense of humor. Directly across the street from the main entrance to Chinatown, the Triton's garishly painted lobby announces its presence with authority. The rooms include ecosuites, with biodegradable linens and special air-filtration systems. Other suites have been dedicated to California rock stars, including Graham Nash, Jerry Garcia, and Carlos Santana. Nash's room is called "Suite: Judy Blue Eyes," while Santana's is the "Black Magic Bedroom." Expensive.

The Orchard Hotel
665 Bush Street
362–8878
www.theorchardhotel.com
Modern, attractive rooms come complete with DVD player, CD player, and large television. The Orchard is for those who want luxury with high-tech appointments. Expensive.

Places to Eat Downtown

Four Seas
731 Grant Avenue
989–8188
www.fourseas.com
Four Seas is a good place to indulge in a leisurely dim sum meal. Chinatown's claimed oldest restaurant, opened in 1960, it boasts a great bird's-eye view of the neighborhood if you can score a window seat. Open Monday through Friday 11:00 A.M. to 9:30 P.M., Saturday and Sunday 9:00 A.M. to 9:30 P.M. Moderate.

Sam's Grill
374 Bush Street
421–0594
One of downtown's best old-school joints open weekdays only, Sam's opened in 1867. It's not quite as well-known to outsiders as is the famed Tadich, and its customers tend to be extremely loyal. They have to be, because one of the restaurant's hallmarks is service that can only be described as charmingly rude. Remember, they don't hate you, that's just the way they are. Sam's specializes in seafood, and everything is best enjoyed in one of the train-compartment booths, where you can pull the curtain closed for privacy. Open Monday through Friday 11:00 A.M. to 9:00 P.M. Moderate.

Schroeder's
240 Front Street
421–4778
www.schroederssf.com
The Financial District is full of throwback restaurants that attract generation after generation. The most amusing of these is Schroeder's, a German beer hall with bawdy murals on the walls, polka bands each weekend evening, and Teutonic-accented waitresses in Bavarian dresses. If you find yourself scratching your head at the sign that says LUNCH FOR MEN AND WOMEN, realize that the restaurant only recently started serving the fairer sex. Expect lots of sausage, sauerkraut, and—naturally—beer. Open Monday through Friday 11:00 A.M. to 9:00 P.M., Saturday 4:30 to 9:00 P.M. Moderate.

Tadich Grill
240 California Street
391–1849
Opened as soon as the gold miners started pouring off the boats in 1849, Tadich Grill is California's oldest restaurant. Its long counter fills with Financial District suits enjoying burgers and steaks each afternoon and evening. Adding to the historical effect is the California Street cable car, which still rumbles past the restaurant, ringing its bell. Open Monday through Friday 11:00 A.M. to 9:30 P.M., Saturday 11:30 A.M. to 9:30 P.M. Moderate.

North Beach and the Waterfront

For starters, there is no beach in North Beach. There once was, before the land-filling began during the Gold Rush years, when shallow Yerba Buena Cove crept all the way to Montgomery Street. The outdated name seems appropriate for a neighborhood that clings so tightly to its past. Perhaps no part of the city better exemplifies San Francisco and its charms than North Beach. To the east, Telegraph Hill, rife with quaint little alleys and stairways down to the bay, ascends mightily. To the west, cable cars are pulled up and down the steep slopes of ritzy Russian Hill. In the valley between is the heart of North Beach, an entertaining stretch of shops, cafes, bars, and restaurants that feels the most European of any of the city's districts. Historically San Francisco's Little Italy, North Beach has seen its Italian population drop from 80,000 in the middle of the twentieth century to around 8,000, but the cultural imprint remains. Over the years North Beach has blended with Chinatown, and the popularity of the area has raised rents and caused the inevitable gentrification. Still, when sipping an espresso and digging into a rich slice of tiramisu while glancing at that day's Italian sports pages, you could be forgiven for thinking yourself in Rome.

Even as the population has changed, the neighborhood has clung fiercely to its roots, scuttling any attempts to install

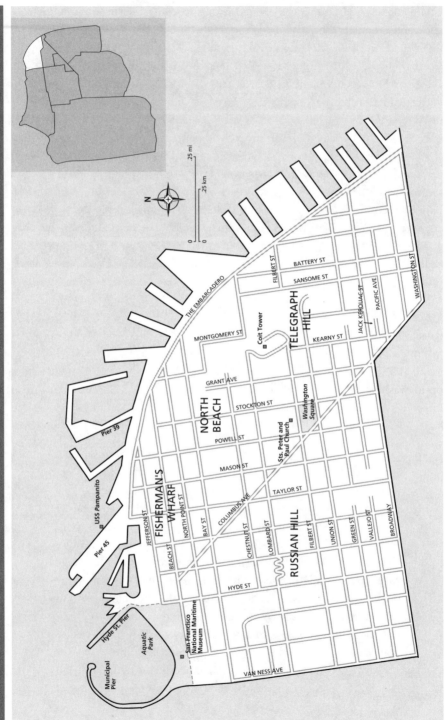

N

.25 mi

.25 km

THE EMBARCADERO

FILBERT ST

BATTERY ST

SANSOME ST

PACIFIC AVE

WASHINGTON ST

JACK KEROUAC ST

Coit Tower

TELEGRAPH HILL

KEARNY ST

Montgomery St

GRANT AVE

NORTH BEACH

STOCKTON ST

Washington Square

POWELL ST

Sts. Peter and Paul Church

MASON ST

FISHERMAN'S WHARF

TAYLOR ST

Pier 39

COLUMBUS AVE

BAY ST

JEFFERSON ST

NORTH POINT ST

CHESTNUT ST

LOMBARD ST

RUSSIAN HILL

FILBERT ST

UNION ST

GREEN ST

VALLEJO ST

BROADWAY

USS Pampanito

BEACH ST

Pier 45

HYDE ST

Hyde St. Pier

San Francisco National Maritime Museum

VAN NESS AVE

Aquatic Park

Municipal Pier

chain stores among the family-owned shops. Keeping the Italian heritage front and center remains a priority, from the red, white, and green stripes painted on the neighborhood's utility poles to the signs identifying Columbus Avenue, North Beach's main drag, as "Corso Cristoforo Colombo." And despite the changes, you are still likely to hear a knot of older men in the park commenting in Italian on the legs of female passersby or two young men in track suits discussing the fate of Milan's soccer teams.

On the block of Stockton Street where the lampposts' painted tricolors change from Chinese Nationalist blue, white, and red to the Italian red, white, and green, is the **North Beach Museum** (1435 Stockton Street), a space devoted to preserving the artifacts of North Beach the way it was. Hidden inside the US Bank branch, the museum has a rich collection of historical photos. Some, like the myriad school photos, are purely quaint nostalgia, but others are of more general interest. Shots of traditional felucca fishing boats and proud proprietors beaming in front of bygone shops give an idea of what the neighborhood once was. A picture of local boys Frankie Corsetti, Tony Lazzeri, and a young Joe DiMaggio, all in their New York Yankee uniforms, shows the pride North Beach took in its baseball stars. Most affecting, though, are the few prints taken in the days following the 1906 earthquake, when most of the neighborhood was either in rubble or in flames. The sheer devastation is obvious in the photos of Telegraph Hill with nearly every lot flattened or the jam-packed tent city that sprang up in Washington Square for the newly homeless families. The museum's main mission is to preserve the neighborhood's heritage, but it also acknowledges the ways it has changed, as in exhibits dedicated to the Chinese families whose lives were spent on these streets, and a poignant poem, handwritten in the 1970s by Lawrence Ferlinghetti, called "The Old Italians Dying." The museum's hours are the same as the bank's: Monday through Thursday 9:00 A.M. to 5:00 P.M., Friday 9:00 A.M. to 6:00 P.M., Saturday 9:00 A.M. to 1:00 P.M. Call 391–6210.

Walking up Columbus Avenue from the Transamerica Pyramid, you can tell exactly where the Financial District ends and North Beach begins. When you

TOP ATTRACTIONS IN NORTH BEACH AND THE WATERFRONT

City Lights Bookstore	Telegraph Hill
Steps of Rome	Fisherman's Wharf
Washington Square	USS *Pampanito*

stop seeing office towers and start seeing bars and cafes, you might feel your-self relaxing instinctively. One of the first places along the avenue is the **San Francisco Brewing Company** (155 Columbus Avenue), at the corner of Pacific Avenue, one of the country's oldest brewpubs. The current establishment opened in 1985, but the building's legacy as a watering hole dates back to 1907 and the Barbary Coast days. Originally called the Andromeda Saloon, it was one of many bars in what was then a hard-edged neighborhood, a notorious gath-ering place for sailors, prostitutes, and businessmen who in those days passed for respectable. Rough as the crowd may have been, there probably wasn't too much trouble at the Andromeda in 1913, at least. That was when Jack Dempsey, future heavyweight champion of the world, worked there as a bouncer.

Most of the old Barbary Coast saloons disappeared with Prohibition, but the Andromeda survived by renaming itself a "cafe" and officially serving clams and oysters instead of alcoholic libations. Although it is rumored that the FBI finally put the shackles on Baby Face Nelson, then Public Enemy Number One, here in 1939, the Andromeda eventually drifted into obscurity, and many coats of paint over the years hid the original fixtures.

Thanks to a restoration in the late 1970s, much of the building's Barbary Coast glory is once again visible. Sit at the original mahogany bar and contem-plate the characters who once took drinks there. Having trouble conjuring up the image? Look down at the white-tiled spit trough in the floor next to your stool. The proprietor, brewmaster Allan Paul, is proud of its authenticity, although he doesn't suggest you employ it. Also adding to the ambience are the 1916 punkah fans spinning vertically like waterwheels overhead. The palm branch arms are pushed around by a contraption of motors and leather belts. Numerous tasty beers are all brewed on the premises, using a system of tubes running from the copper tank in the back room down to the basement's giant kegs from which your fresh pint is pulled. Food, such as burgers and salads, is also served. Tours and explanations are happily given upon request. Open daily from noon to 1:00 A.M. Call 434-3344 or visit www.sfbrewing.com. Inexpensive.

A stroll farther up Columbus brings you to a more modern bit of San Fran-cisco history. The blocks near Broadway belonged to the writers of the beat movement, and several of the alleys they haunted now bear their names. On the south corner of Columbus and Jack Kerouac Street, **Vesuvio Cafe** (225 Colum-bus Avenue) seems not to have changed much at all since the *On the Road* author was a regular. The walls are covered with beat memorabilia, and the stools are covered with characters who probably haven't left since those days. While Vesuvio clearly trades on its literary past to attract beat acolytes—serving drinks like the Jack Kerouac, a tequila and rum concoction, and Bohemian coffee—there is a certain authenticity to it as well. Food is not served. Open daily from 6:00 to 2:00 A.M. Call 362–3370 or visit www.vesuvio.com.

Vesuvio opened in 1948, but its reputation was enhanced in 1953 when **City Lights Bookstore** (261 Columbus Avenue) opened on the other side of what is now Jack Kerouac Street. As the epicenter of the movement, it is still the holiest site on the beat pilgrimage. Lawrence Ferlinghetti, the poet and patron saint of the beats, opened the shop in 1953 to complement his small literary magazine, and the store quickly gained notoriety as the place to be. Much of this was due to Ferlinghetti's decision in 1955 to publish his friend Allen Ginsberg's *Howl,* a book that mainstream publishers considered too explicit and controversial to touch. City Lights became the place to get your hands on the stuff the powers that be didn't want you reading and your best bet for encountering so-called beatniks. The building still has a homemade feel, with narrow staircases and chairs that are a collapse waiting to happen, and it is the kind of place where you could sit and read an entire book without anyone even knowing you were there. The store now carries a full selection of mainstream books, but the section that makes it special is the poetry room on the top floor, with its definitive collection of verse from the beat era to today, much of it first published by Ferlinghetti, and Ferlinghetti's own oil paintings. Open daily from 10:00 A.M. to midnight. Call 362–8193 or visit www.citylights.com.

On the other side of Columbus is **Tosca Cafe** (242 Columbus Avenue), one of San Francisco's classiest and most beloved bars. From the moment you walk in the door, it's clear that you are in a different kind of place, the sort of joint where you ought to be hanging up your fur coat or tilting a felt hat at the bartender. The classic jukebox is filled with Italian arias, the bar is polished, the red vinyl booths are inviting, and the clientele is often San Francisco's A-list. On a cold day, Tosca's signature drink, the house cappuccino, is a godsend. It's not coffee—rather a mixture of brandy, hot chocolate, and steamed milk—

AUTHORS' FAVORITES IN NORTH BEACH AND THE WATERFRONT

Tosca Cafe

Steps of Rome

Eating Liguria Bakery's focaccia in Washington Square

Filbert Steps

Hanging off the side of the Powell-Hyde cable car

but it will pick you up. Even if you don't intend to order one, you may be enticed by the rows and rows of them along the bar waiting to be completed. Don't be surprised if you spot someone like Francis Ford Coppola or Sean Penn at one of the booths, or the mayor and a few supervisors. Despite being a favorite of the powerful, Tosca has recently developed something of an outlaw reputation. Owner Jeannette Etheredge has openly flouted a California law banning smoking in bars. So far, no punishment has been meted out, showing the benefit of having prominent patrons. Open daily from 5:00 P.M. to 2:00 A.M. Call 986–9651.

North Beach could well be called the espresso district, considering the number of cafes that serve up quality cups of the strong stuff. The one that started the trend is *Caffe Trieste* (609 Vallejo Street). To get there, cross Broadway and turn right on Vallejo, passing the line of parked motorcycles and mopeds. Opened in 1956, Trieste is said to have been the first coffeehouse to serve up espresso on the West Coast. There are at least ten other places to get a good espresso in the neighborhood, but Trieste remains a popular hangout because of its casual atmosphere and its feeling of history. A favorite spot for bohemian poetry readings in the 1950s and 1960s, regulars now come for the Saturday afternoon (approximately 2:00 P.M.) concerts of traditional Italian songs sung by the Giotta family, who founded and still own the cafe. Open Sunday through Thursday from 6:30 A.M. to 11:00 P.M., Friday and Saturday until 11:00 P.M. Call 982–2605 or visit www.caffetrieste.com. Inexpensive.

In contrast to Caffe Trieste's laid-back atmosphere, *Steps of Rome* (348 Columbus Avenue) is constantly abuzz, with Italian pop music blaring and the entirely Italian staff continuously bantering with one another. It starts as you walk by: The man out front will try anything he can to cajole you into coming in and sitting down. Be warned, if you as much as acknowledge his efforts, he will probably hook you. The restaurant serves a full menu of pretty tasty Italian fare, but feel free to stop in for a coffee, an aperitif, or dessert and just watch the scene. Of all the places aspiring to Italian-ness in North Beach, Steps of Rome probably captures a certain aspect of it most effectively. A contingent of young Italian men seems to linger outside the cafe at all hours, leaning on their Vespas and generally "making the scene." Playful flirtation is the norm from the staff, and they are not above chiding you for not eating enough, not ordering a second drink, or being late to meet a date. This is an establishment comfortable with its silliness, which always makes it fun, and it hops well into the night. Open Sunday through Thursday 8:30 A.M. to 2:00 A.M., Friday and Saturday to 3:00 A.M. Call 397–0435 or visit www.stepsofrome.com. Inexpensive.

At the heart of North Beach, where Columbus meets Union and Filbert Streets, is *Washington Square,* a park used for snacking, sleeping, and chatting.

In the early mornings it is dominated by elderly Chinese men and women practicing t'ai chi; in the late afternoons the yuppies and their dogs take over. Bounded on the west by the diagonally running Columbus Avenue, the park is not quite square—but it used to be. Imagine the fenced-off triangle containing a pond and statuary on the other side of the impertinent avenue as the fourth corner. This once was so, before the city built Columbus Avenue as a direct thoroughfare for residents of the burgeoning waterfront districts who commuted to the Financial District. The park's importance as a gathering place was never more evident than in the weeks following the 1906 earthquake, when residents of this particularly ravaged neighborhood pitched tents here because their homes had been destroyed.

In the park's center stands a statue of a proud-looking man in colonial garb. Given the park's name, you'd be forgiven for assuming it to be the first president. In fact, it is Ben Franklin, and the statue is actually just the top of a temperance fountain. The idea, almost certainly a failure, was for people to drink water instead of liquor. The fountain, one of many in different towns in northern California, was commissioned by H. G. Cogswell, a dentist who made a killing in the Gold Rush and was devoted to the temperance movement. Especially in those days, San Franciscans were not particularly protemperance, even though Cogswell's fountain is etched with the claim that one of the spigots dispensed the high-class water from the Vichy region of France. Not bloody likely.

The park's other sculpture is the *Volunteer Fire Fighters Memorial* next to Columbus Avenue. Haig Patigian, a prominent San Francisco sculptor in the 1930s, created the three life-size fire fighters with courageous looks on their faces, one of them carrying a woman. The statue was built in the name of Lillian Hitchcock Coit, a celebrated eccentric of her time with a deep love for fire fighters. Her family moved to San Francisco in 1851, a time when buildings were put up hastily and haphazardly, and the city was ravaged by fire on a regular basis. At the age of nine, while playing in an abandoned building that went up in flames, she was rescued by the volunteer fire fighters of Knickerbocker Engine Company No. 5. Little Lillie became a lifelong devotee of the company and an unofficial patroness of the fire department. As a child, Lillian was known for running after fire engines when the alarms sounded, exhorting men on the streets to pitch in and help put out the flames. The men of Knickerbocker No. 5 adored her in return and, in 1863 named her an honorary member. During city parades she could always be seen waving from the top of engine No. 5. Also known for dressing like a man to gain access to some of the less ladylike parts of the city, she was a regular at a few poker games. Lillian later married Howard Coit, a wealthy stock trader, and spent much of her adult life traveling the world. When she died in 1929, she left one-third of her considerable estate "for the purpose of adding beauty to the city I have always loved." Part of the money was used to build this memorial, and the rest went to the more famous Coit Tower, visible behind the monument.

As the center of Italian life in San Francisco, it stands to reason that North Beach would need a prominent Catholic church. Fitting the bill nicely is the white ***Saints Peter and Paul Church*** (666 Filbert Street), a combination Romanesque and Byzantine structure across Filbert Street from Washington Square whose twin 191-foot turrets dominate the skyline of North Beach. Begun in 1912, it was not finished until 1924. (The unfinished building was used as a backdrop in Cecil B. DeMille's 1923 epic, *The Ten Commandments*.) The church's prized possession is a 40-foot-tall marble and onyx altar carved in Italy, shipped to San Francisco in pieces, and reassembled inside. While the church still wears its Italian roots proudly, bearing a quote from Dante along the facade, it is also a testament to the way the neighborhood has changed. Nearly all of the uniformed kids attending the church school today are of Asian descent, and Sunday Mass is held in English, Italian, and Chinese. Call 421–0809.

North Beach is typically most crowded at night, but one reason to visit early in the day is ***Liguria Bakery*** (1700 Stockton Street), on the corner of Filbert and Stockton Streets. Liguria sells one thing: focaccia. The flat Italian bread comes in four varieties—plain, raisin, onion, and pizza—and when the day's supply is gone, the shop closes. The same family has made and sold the focaccia since the place opened in 1911 and has built an army of devoted customers. There are few better ways to spend a sunny San Francisco morning than munching on a bag of the stuff on a bench in the square. The bakery's official hours are Monday through Friday 8:00 A.M. to 2:00 P.M., Saturday 7:00 A.M. to 2:00 P.M., and Sunday 7:00 A.M. to noon, but, as a testament to the quality of its product, it almost never stays open that long. Call 421–3786.

The sustenance will come in handy if you plan to scale Filbert Street to the heights of ***Telegraph Hill,*** a mostly residential area with excellent views of the city and the bay. It was these views, in fact, that made it critical to early San Franciscans and gave the hill its name. The hill's highest point is atop Filbert Street, and standing there you have clear sight lines to the Golden Gate, San Pablo Bay, downtown, and almost all of the areas of the old Barbary Coast. Because of this fortuitous view, spotters were stationed here during Gold Rush days to watch for ships coming into the bay from the Pacific or south from the Gold Country's rivers. The spotters determined the ships' cargo and then used a semaphore system to relay the news to people on lower ground. This "telegraph" system told residents anxious for supplies from the east whether to expect food, clothing, building materials, or other items, so that they could decide whether to head down to the piers.

The advent of the electric telegraph machine rendered the semaphore system unnecessary, and city leaders were looking for a use for the well-placed land. When the aforementioned Lillian Hitchcock Coit died in 1929, a city commission elected to build *Coit Tower* as a monument in her honor. A persistent myth holds that the tower's design is that of a fire hose nozzle, fitting with Lillie's devotion. It really does seem plausible, but alas, architect Arthur Brown Jr., who also planned City Hall, had nothing of the sort in mind. He simply found the nozzlelike shape attractive.

By all means, take a trip to the top ($3.75) for the spectacular views, but don't forget to have a (free) look around the ground floor at the murals that cover the walls. When the tower was completed in 1933, the walls were bare; the city didn't have the money, at the height of the Great Depression, to commission their decoration. When President Franklin Roosevelt's Works Progress Administration made money available for public art, the city's Arts Commission pounced, and began taking design submissions from local artists for murals depicting California life in the 1930s. Twenty-five designs were chosen, and the artists set to work creating different representative scenes. Given the tough times, many of the images are somber, such as the agrarian family with no food on their plates, and bankers staring at a graph showing the precipitous drop in the stock market. Many are quite playful though, and they give an idea of the fun the artists had while working together in the tight spaces. Several used the other artists as models for their work and embedded subtle inside jokes in the pictures.

The artwork also created considerable controversy over some of its political content. The 1930s were a time of great labor unrest in San Francisco, and fear of communism was considerable. Thus, murals showing stern-faced workers assembled in a disciplined mass, newsstands displaying the *Daily Worker,* and library patrons reading Karl Marx rankled many of the city elites who attended a preview of the murals in August 1934. The Arts Commission allowed these images to stay up, but one piece was judged to have crossed the line. Above the west-facing windows, between his depictions of the steelworker and the surveyor, Clifford Wright had drawn, among other symbols, a hammer and sickle with the words "workers of the world unite." When the building opened officially in October, the offending image had been removed, and the space remains blank today. Open daily, 10:00 A.M. to 6:00 P.M. Call 362–0808 or visit www.coittower.org. City Guides offers a free tour of the murals every Saturday morning at 11:00, which includes access to some not normally open to the public. The well-informed guides can also tell you all of the quirky facts about the drawings.

There is not much else to see on Telegraph Hill, but the trip down to the waterfront is an interesting attraction in itself. Turn right as you exit the tower and walk along the road a few paces until you see steps heading down to the left. This is the top of the **Filbert Steps,** 381 stairs built along the steep edge of the hill. The steps wind through an unlikely area of attractive houses perched on a hillside too steep for roads. For the residents here, the steps are the only way to get to their homes, and you will likely see a few of them indefatigably climbing up with bags of groceries. If that looks tiring, imagine trying to move in. They seem to have enough energy left to maintain the steps and the trees that surround them, however. As a favor to them, stay on the main path or you might accidentally wander into someone's yard.

thesealionsof pier39

Pier 39, just to the east of Fisherman's Wharf, is an assemblage of snack shops, kitschy stores, and tourist traps, resembling a shopping mall on the water. One nice attraction there, however, arrived through no intent of the designers. Just west of the pier's tip is a series of wooden docks that since 1989 have become the favorite haunt for the bay's sea lion population.

Before that year, sea lions mostly "hauled out" of the water near Seal Rock on the city's west side, but since then, they have begun turning up in ever greater numbers at Pier 39's K Dock. Some have opined that the 1989 earthquake changed their habits, but marine biologists have not been able to prove it.

During the winter months, it is typical to see up to 900 of the pleasant-looking creatures lying on top of one another on the docks. Crowds ignore the shopping and instead watch and laugh as the sea lions basically lie around, keep each other warm, and make funny noises. On winter weekends, Marine Mammal Center volunteers are available to answer tourists' questions.

Any city that attracts floods of tourists must have an area that seems designed to overstimulate them with tacky displays and to unceremoniously separate them from their spending money. In San Francisco, **Fisherman's Wharf** is that place. The area's main retail commerce is made up of wax museums, theme restaurants, and shops selling T-shirts proclaiming, "I Escaped from Alcatraz." The sidewalks are populated by men covered in silver paint, three-card-monte dealers and their painfully obvious shills, and "Bushman," a fellow who, despite lawsuits, leaps from behind his handheld shrubbery on Jefferson Street to scare the daylights out of unsuspecting Midwesterners. Given this state of affairs, it is not surprising that most San Franciscans avoid the neighborhood at all costs. There is another side to the wharf though, one that gets lost in the glare of the midway. Adjacent to Pier 39 is another real attraction (besides the famous sea lions), the **Aquarium of the Bay.** The highlight is moving through two 30-foot tubes via a mechanical walkway, with bay aquatic life swimming on the other side of the plastic lining. Open daily 10:00 A.M. to 6:00 P.M, and to 7:00 P.M. in summer. Admission is $12.95 for adults and $6.50 for children under twelve. Call (888) 732-3483 or visit www.aquariumofthebay.com. This is still the center of San Francisco's fishing industry, a living monument to the mostly Italian sailors who historically plied the San Francisco Bay.

To avoid the schlock and head straight for the good stuff, hop off the trolley at **Pier 45,** an array of warehouses, docks, and seafood restaurants. During the day the area is filled mostly with tourists and diners, but in the predawn hours the place really comes to life when fishermen sell their catch to retailers. Historically, the San Francisco fishing industry was dominated by Italian immigrants, most of them from coastal areas of Liguria and Calabria. In the early part of the century, they set sail from the area around Pier 45 in small wooden boats called feluccas, plying the rich bay. The local merchants' association has recently made an effort to clean up the area and has put up a series of signs noting its history and directing a short walking tour.

The area in front of Pier 45 is lined with outdoor seafood stands with small seating areas. During the winter months, when the signature Dungeness crab is in season, you can plop yourself on a stool and order a crab cocktail that you know is fresh, because you saw the crab crawling around and snapping its claws a minute ago. Each stand is owned by the sit-down restaurant behind it, and part of the fun is in watching the greeters at each door compete for business, each one explaining why the establishment next door is no good and you should eat at his place instead.

Among the warehouses and restaurants, just behind the main docking area, is the **Fishermen's and Seamen's Chapel.** This simple wood structure, unassuming on the end of a wooden pier, was built in 1979 to honor the more than

Fishermen's and Seamen's Chapel

200 fishermen lost at sea since the early 1900s. The names of the dead, most of them Italian, are inscribed on plaques covering the walls. The building is closed except during services, which are open to the public. If you're there on a sunny Sunday morning, go for the Latin Mass. You might not understand a thing, but the windows behind the preacher look out on the Golden Gate— where the Pacific Ocean meets the San Francisco Bay—and the famous red bridge that spans it, a spiritual sight if there ever was one. On the first weekend in October, the chapel holds its Madonna del Lume Celebration, a sixty-year tradition of blessing the fleet of fishing boats. Named for the patroness of fishermen, the ritual was brought by immigrants from the Sicilian town of Porticello. The weekend involves a special memorial service at sea, a parade of fishing boats, High Mass delivered in Italian at the chapel, and a procession in which an icon of the Madonna is held aloft.

On the bay side of Pier 45, behind the large gray fish-processing plants, the *USS* **Pampanito**, a World War II submarine, has been turned into a museum for the navy's often overlooked "silent service." The *Pampanito* made tours throughout the Pacific, from Hawaii to Australia to New Guinea, sinking six Japanese ships along the way. Admission to the sub includes a headset with a self-guided tour that adds greatly to the experience. The recording features the voices of several men who served on the ship, describing everything from their dramatic operations to the mundane business of preparing food and bathing under tight conditions. And conditions were certainly tight. Once you head through the hatch, it might seem crowded with twenty or so fellow tourists. Then try to imagine a crew of as many as eighty sailors trying to live aboard for months at a time. Unbelievably, the crew once had to add seventy-three more men to its crowded complement when they rescued a group of British and Australian POWs swimming from a sunken Japanese boat. You can hear the ex-sailors' smiles through the recorder as they recount the POWs' response to the rescue. "You bloody Yanks," they recall hearing, "First you sink us, then you save us."

Even without the extra guests, the men were obviously forced to get closely acquainted. Bunks were traded off, with about two for every three sailors, and many had to sleep above or beneath the torpedoes. Moving between compartments of the craft meant squeezing yourself through a hatch about 3 feet high. The hatches are still the way through today, and because the sub floats in open water, waves keep it rocking, adding a certain element of realism. The *Pampanito* returned in one piece, but fifty-two of the American submarines that went on tours during World War II never made it back to port. The *Pampanito* serves as a floating memorial to 3,505 men who perished at sea during that conflict. Open from 9:00 A.M. to 8:00 P.M., and Sunday through

Thursday from 9:00 A.M. to 6:00 P.M. Admission is $7.00 for adults, $4.00 for children under thirteen. Call 561–6662 or 775–1943 or visit www.maritime.org/hours.html for more information.

On exiting Pier 45, turn right and walk about four blocks along Jefferson Street to reach **San Francisco Maritime National Historic Park.** The well-maintained area has a museum, classic ships at Hyde Street Pier, a green patch of grass surrounding the cable car turnaround, and **Aquatic Park,** a short beach whose waters are protected from the bay by the curved Municipal Pier. This is an area designed for swimming, and for many neighborhood kids and adults alike, it serves as the local pool. Before you strip down and dive in, keep in mind that the waters are not exactly tropical. San Francisco has quite a few hardy souls, however, and on most days someone will be there working out his or her stroke. None of them can match the fearlessness shown in 1915, when, as part of the Panama Pacific International Exposition, Harry Houdini escaped from a manacled box lowered into Aquatic Park's water. Next to Aquatic Park are the **Dolphin Club** and the **South End Rowing Club,** which organize swimming events. Both are open to the public a few days a week, but make sure you know which one you are in. The two clubs, each more than one hundred years old, have a historic rivalry, so you wouldn't want to insult anyone.

Pier 45 Shed A

Shed A provides temporary quarters to the Musée Méchanique, 170 coin-operated machines that tell fortunes, show old pictures, or test the strength of any comer. Many date from the 1880s, and none is more famous than the huge and raucous Laughing Sal, which screeches and cackles almost constantly. When I was four years old, I always begged for quarters to make one of the slightly menacing woman fortune-tellers foretell my fortune—even though I couldn't read it yet. Nowadays a quarter doesn't go as far, but it still scores me a cryptic fortune on a tiny piece of colored paper that is open to interpretation! The Musée Méchanique was housed below the Cliff House for years. A few years ago that landmark's restoration required the long-time owner-operator to move. The Musée's threatened closure because of financial difficulties led to a huge public outcry and calls for support. Its open-ended reprieve at Fisherman's Wharf Pier 45 in the old shed across from the USS *Pampanito* delights children and adults alike. Open Monday through Friday 10:00 A.M. to 7:00 P.M., and to 8:00 P.M. on weekends. Call 346–2000. There are also a few exhibits from the unofficial Museum of the City of San Francisco, another institution searching for a permanent home.

—M.C.

Beyond Alcatraz

OK, so everyone knows about "The Rock." But take a look at the big island right behind it. That's *Angel Island,* and it can make for a more fun and informative trip.

Angel Island is in many ways the Ellis Island of the West, where hundreds of thousands of Asian immigrants were processed. Between 1910 and 1940 some 175,000 Chinese immigrants were detained in the North Garrison, waiting for their visa requests to come through. Those were the days of the exclusion laws, restrictive quotas designed specifically to limit the numbers of Asians in the United States. The North Garrison building is now a museum to Chinese immigration, and as you walk through the halls you can see Chinese characters carved into the walls by people who were detained for several months.

Before becoming a state park in the 1950s, Angel Island was long a military fort considered critical to the defense of San Francisco Bay. During World War II, more than 300,000 soldiers were processed on the island before shipping out to the Pacific. Nowadays, Angel Island is also known for its great recreation. Bike the perimeter road, kayak around the island and its many coves, hike to the top of 781-foot Mount Livermore, or just picnic on the beach. Visit www.angelisland.org for more information.

Blue and Gold Fleet at Pier 41 runs one ferry to the island each morning and back each afternoon, with additional trips on the summer schedule. Call 705–5555 or visit www.blueandgoldfleet.com for a schedule and reservations.

Just above Aquatic Park is the ***San Francisco Maritime Museum*** (900 Beach Street at the foot of Polk Street), home to fascinating artifacts and explanations of the history of seafaring in San Francisco. Much attention is focused on the Gold Rush days, when hundreds of ships came pouring into San Francisco Bay. In most cases, once the ships dropped anchor, the entire crew quickly came ashore and headed for the gold mines. With no one left to sail them, the ships were converted into floating warehouses, inns, and whatever else was needed. Among these ships was the *Niantic,* which arrived in San Francisco in 1849 after a long voyage from New England via Cape Horn. After nearly everyone aboard headed for the hills, it served as a storehouse until it burned in the fire of 1851 and sank into the bay. The ship, like many others, was forgotten as the bay was filled in around it. In 1977, during construction on Clay Street near the Transamerica Pyramid, workers digging the foundation discovered the *Niantic,* which apparently was a high-class warehouse: Among the things unearthed with the ship were cases of French champagne and labels from Belgian pâté jars. A 15-foot-long hunk of the ship's stern, made of wood with metal siding, sits in the museum lobby.

The museum also has early daguerreotypes of San Francisco before the landfill started and several colorfully painted figureheads from historic ships. An exhibit on ships' radios features a radar display showing the ships on the bay that day and a pair of headphones allowing you to listen live to the Coast Guard traffic cops moving ships around. The top floor is also a good place for ship watching, and a book showing pictures of different types of craft helps you know what you're looking at. Open daily 10:00 A.M. to 5:00 P.M. Admission is free. Call 561–7100 or visit www.nps.gov/safr or www.maritime.org.

About a fifteen-minute walk along the east side of Russian Hill brings you to the **San Francisco Art Institute** (800 Chestnut Street), which has been educating artists since the 1800s. The building, which looks like a medieval Italian castle, is impeccably located, with views of Telegraph Hill and Coit Tower to the east, North Beach below and to the south, and the bay to the west. Walk to the back of the building and you are at the rooftop cafe, where students with piercings and torn clothing drink beer and coffee, somewhat oblivious to the gorgeous vistas. The main draw is the Diego Rivera gallery. Rivera's residency in the 1930s brought international recognition to the school, and his 1931 mural *The Making of a Fresco Showing the Building of a City,* which covers one wall, is a great example of his work. The complex piece shows Rivera himself working on a mural, which depicts workers assembling skyscrapers among other things. The resulting trompe l'oeil effect leaves it unclear which of the people in it are building the city and which are helping to make the fresco. It is one of three Rivera murals in San Francisco, and the only one always open to the public (daily 8:00 A.M. to 8:00 P.M.). Admission is free. Call 771–7020 or visit www.sanfranciscoart.edu/dr.htm.

iwanttobeinthat number

If, when walking the streets of North Beach, you see a brass band in black suits and hats leading what appears to be a funeral procession, you haven't accidentally wandered into New Orleans. You have encountered the *Green Street Mortuary Band.*

The majority Chinese population of North Beach has a tradition of brass bands leading funeral marches, and the Green Street Mortuary (649 Green Street) is happy to oblige. The band is usually a ten-piece assemblage with a rotating list of players, many of whom are moonlighting from professional orchestras.

Walk down Chestnut to familiar Columbus Avenue to find **Bimbo's 365 Club** (1025 Columbus Avenue), one of San Francisco's best venues for live music and a throwback to the 1930s. In 1931, when Agostino (Bimbo) Giuntoli, an immigrant from Tuscany, first opened his club at 365 Market Street, the

Depression was in full swing, but there was still room for a successful speakeasy. San Franciscans tired of being depressed filled the club, drinking gin from coffee cups and watching Bimbo's famous chorus line. Among the girls was one Rita Cansino, who later gained fame as Rita Hayworth. Bimbo's was also famous as the home of Dolfina, the Girl in the Fishbowl. Apparently some sort of optical illusion, there actually appeared to be a naked girl swimming in a giant fishbowl behind the bar. Today a mural pays homage to Dolfina. The club moved to the fringes of North Beach in 1951 and stayed popular by presenting different types of acts each night. The events are still eclectic, with British rock one night, a swing band the next, and '70s funk the night after. Above all, the atmosphere is great, from the art deco furnishings to the sitting room with plush seating. Bimbo's is sometimes closed for private parties, but check the local papers for events. Light snacks are available. Call 474–0365 for show listings or visit www.bimbos365club.com. Inexpensive.

Places to Stay
North Beach and
the Waterfront

Hotel Boheme
444 Columbus Avenue
433–9111
www.hotelboheme.com
This old-world hotel is right in the heart of North Beach, and its decor pays tribute to the beats and bohemians who once defined the neighborhood. The hotel opened in 1995, but the building dates back to 1906, and the spirit is definitely that of the past. Moderate.

San Remo Hotel
2237 Mason Street
776–8688
www.sanremohotel.com
The San Remo opened just after the earthquake in 1906. The hotel is a bit like an Italian pension, with shared bathrooms and no

telephones or televisions in the room. The rooms are small but comfortable. Inexpensive.

Washington Square Inn
1660 Stockton Street
981–4220
www.washingtonsquareinn sf.com
This European-style bed-and-breakfast is right on Washington Square. An added perk is the daily wine and cheese served in the quaint dining room. Moderate.

The Wharf Inn
2601 Mason Street
673–7411
www.wharfinn.com
This simple inn is well located right on the cable car line near Fisherman's Wharf. Keep in mind that the cables run until 1:00 A.M., so you might hear a rumbling. There is also a penthouse suite with two bedrooms and a large living room for groups. Moderate.

Places to Eat
North Beach and
the Waterfront

Café Niebaum-Coppola
916 Kearny Street
291–1799
www.cafecoppola.com
Francis Ford Coppola has installed a panini, pizza, pasta, and calzone cafe on the ground floor of his green-colored Sentinel Building. Upstairs is American Zoetrope, his film production company. Open Tuesday through Friday 10:00 A.M. to 10:00 P.M., Saturday noon to 10:00 P.M., Sunday to 9:00 P.M. Moderate.

Caffe Sport
574 Green Street
981–1251
Eating at Caffe Sport is an experience. The tables are covered in wild tile patterns, the walls are filled with

strange stuff, including wood carvings by the owner himself, and the service is almost universally rude. They get away with it though, because the Sicilian-style seafood dishes are spectacular. Look at the insulting waiters as part of the entertainment. Open Tuesday through Saturday noon to 2:00 P.M. and 5:00 to 10:30 P.M. Expensive.

Mario's Bohemian Cigar Store Cafe
566 Columbus Avenue
362–0536
No cigars here! The food is simple, mostly sandwiches and focaccia pizzas, but the atmosphere is what you come for. Located right across from Washington Square, this is a primo place for a snack and a creamy cappuccino. Open Monday through Saturday 10:00 A.M.to midnight, Sunday 10:00 A.M. to 11:00 P.M. Inexpensive.

Molinari's Delicatessen
373 Columbus Avenue
421–2337
www.molinarideli.com
Since 1895, Molinari's has been making ravioli by hand, and importing the best meats, cheeses, and everything else from Italy. There are a few sidewalk tables, but the best thing to do is to grab a sandwich (try the Italian mortadella) and take it to the park. Open Monday through Friday 8:00 A.M. to 6:00 P.M., Saturday 7:30 A.M. to 5:30 P.M. Inexpensive.

U-Lee
1468 Hyde Street
771–9774
Although it is on one of San Francisco's nicest streets, this could fairly be described as a hole in the wall. Don't let the grubby decor turn you away. U-Lee serves some of the best Chinese dishes in the city, and the pot stickers alone are worth a special

trip. Hop off the Powell-Hyde cable car line and you can't miss it. Open Tuesday through Sunday 11:00 A.M. to 9:00 P.M. Inexpensive.

U.S. Restaurant
515 Columbus Avenue
397–5200
OK, this isn't the finest Italian food, but it is an institution, recently reopened after moving from its location down the street where it had been a favorite for more than ninety years. Here you'll find old-style Italian-American dishes like spaghetti and meatballs and veal parmigiana and plenty of cheap Chianti to wash it down. Open Tuesday, Wednesday, Thursday, and Sunday 11:00 A.M. to 9:00 P.M., Friday and Saturday until 10:00 P.M. Inexpensive.

Cow Hollow, the Marina, and the Presidio

Today's **Cow Hollow** is one of San Francisco's fanciest neighborhoods, full of museum-quality dwellings and upscale street life. In its early days, however, when the city was a tiny cluster downtown, Cow Hollow was, as its name suggests, a mostly rural area of dairy farms and slaughterhouses. One thing it did have going for it was a waterfront. Freshwater springs once bubbled up through the area, leading to a series of lagoons north of what is now Union Street. Although the landfill and subsequent development of what is now the Marina District in the early twentieth century took away Cow Hollow's waterfront property, the neighborhood has not suffered for its loss. Nestled at the foot of ritzy Pacific Heights, and just east of the city's biggest park, it's hard to find a more pleasantly located neighborhood. And the water is still just a short walk away.

A good place to start a tour of Cow Hollow is the **Holy Trinity Russian Cathedral** (1520 Green Street) at the corner of Van Ness Avenue. Although this church building was completed in 1909, the congregation dates back to the city's earliest days. In the kind of story that is probably becoming familiar by now, the congregation worshipped in a building downtown until the 1906 quake destroyed it. The best time to walk past the church is 10:00 A.M. on a Sunday, when congregants assemble in

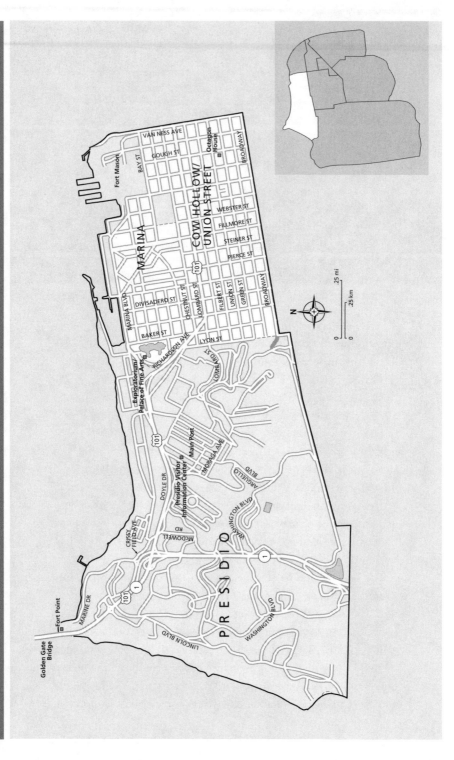

COW HOLLOW, THE MARINA, AND THE PRESIDIO

TOP ATTRACTIONS IN COW HOLLOW, THE MARINA, AND THE PRESIDIO

Union Street	The Palace of Fine Arts
Vedanta Temple	Fort Point National Historic Site

the tower to begin the rhythmic sounding of the parish's seven prized bronze bells. The bells, the largest of which weighs 5,000 pounds, were cast at a Moscow foundry and presented to Holy Trinity as a gift from Czar Alexander III in 1888. The bells also hung at the church's earlier location. By a stroke of luck, they survived the fire that consumed the building: When the quake struck, the bells had been removed from the tower for cleaning. They had another close call in 1999, when an ambitious thief climbed some scaffolding that had been erected for restoration, cut the steel cables that supported them, and made off with three of the smaller bells. The case became a cause célèbre in the local media, and the crook, apparently realizing that his chances of fencing the items were nil, left them on the church's steps late one night. Call 673–8565 or visit www.holy-trinity.org.

An architectural oddity today, the ***Octagon House*** (2645 Gough Street) is one of the few remaining examples of an architectural fad that ran its course a

It's Not Easy Being Green

Most of San Francisco's streets are named for prominent citizens of the city's early days. Many of these men, having come to California to seek their fortunes, likely left behind lives in the east that were not entirely savory. For most, their past indiscretions never found them out west. Talbot H. Green, who gave his name to Cow Hollow's Green Street, was not so lucky.

Green, a wealthy merchant, was one of Gold Rush San Francisco's most prominent citizens, and he decided in 1851 to run for mayor. As his fame grew, some new-comers to the city thought they recognized him as an Eastern man named Paul Geddes, who, after embezzling a large chunk of money, split for the frontier, leaving a wife and four kids behind. Green publicly denied the charges, and boarded a steamer for the East Coast, once again leaving behind a wife and newborn child, ostensibly in order to disprove the claim. The problem was, he really was Paul Geddes. He paid back the money he owed, went back to his first wife, and never returned to San Francisco.

century and a half ago. A fashionable theory in the 1850s and 1860s was that an eight-sided house was better for residents' health, because there were more angles for light to get in (which begs the question, why stop at eight?). About 700 of the houses were built nationwide, and this is one of two surviving in San Francisco. Charles Gough, Cow Hollow's most prominent dairyman, owned the house originally, and the street on which it stands bears his name. Gough (pronounced *goff*) was apparently not one for modesty, taking advantage of his position on the city's naming commission to christen the street in his own honor. Somewhat touchingly, however, he also chose to name the street one block over after his sister Octavia. The Octagon House is now owned by the National Society of Colonial Dames of America, which uses it as a museum of colonial life. The Dames give free tours the second Sunday and second and fourth Thursday of each month. Call 441–7512 for times.

Farther down Green Street, between Webster and Fillmore Streets, is the **Sherman House** (2160 Green Street), once the residence of one of San Francisco's biggest musical patrons and which became one of the finest hotels in the city. Leander Sherman, owner of the West's largest musical instrument shop, called the mansion home for half a century, from 1876 to 1926. He was instrumental in the establishment of San Francisco's opera and symphony companies, and frequently put up musicians on tour in the city. In 1901 Sherman built

Carol Doda's Champagne and Lace Lingerie Boutique

Of all San Francisco's commercial thoroughfares, Union Street is definitely one of the classiest, but in one of its small alleys is a shop that recalls the city's legendary bawdiness. Carol Doda's Champagne and Lace Lingerie Boutique is a tame shop selling various unmentionables, offering little hint of the sensation Ms. Doda once caused throughout San Francisco.

On June 19, 1964, Doda, then a cocktail waitress, scandalized the city by removing her top and entertaining the patrons at the Condor, a bar in North Beach. She was soon a celebrity, with crowds of locals and tourists flocking to the Condor for an eyeful. Two other factors combined to help her make a splash: That very same month, the Republican Party was holding its national convention in San Francisco, guaranteeing her a nightly audience and plenty of press. She also made the acquaintance of a doctor who offered the new service of silicone injections, allowing her to upgrade her assets. Doda soon gained a national reputation and even had her breasts insured by Lloyds of London. Many other topless bars quickly followed, but the Condor remained the most famous, installing a gigantic neon likeness of Doda with her most famous features blinking in the evenings.

AUTHORS' FAVORITES IN COW HOLLOW, THE MARINA, AND THE PRESIDIO

Fort Mason

Lucca Delicatessen

The Exploratorium

The walk along the Golden Gate Promenade to Fort Point

Post Chapel in the Presidio

a grand music room in which his esteemed guests could stage impromptu concerts. As the city's Opera House had not yet been constructed, there was probably no better place to hear the likes of Enrico Caruso or Luisa Tetrazzini belt out an aria or two.

After Sherman's death, the house went through various incarnations, including as a restaurant and a ballet school, none of which was particularly successful. At its lowest point it even had a date with the wrecking ball, until the city designated it a historic landmark. In the late 1970s, the house's fading glory was restored and it was recast as an inn, but it is again closed. It is one of many opulent Victorian- and Edwardian-era buildings, flaunting their gingerbread and frills in Pacific Heights. Lacy, feminine embellishments and, in the 1960s and 1970s, elaborate, sometimes psychedelic paint jobs led a local architectural expert to come up with the term "painted ladies."

Most of Cow Hollow's activity is clustered around **Union Street,** a picturesque shopping strip of Victorian buildings that at night becomes one of the city's most happening spots.

Countless trendy restaurants and bars line Union Street, packing in the well-dressed masses and contending for the most chic reputation. One place that doesn't have to compete is **Perry's** (1944 Union Street), a Cow Hollow institution for thirty-five years. The menu, the entirety of which is painstakingly chalked on a pair of blackboards, never seems to change. Its loyal clientele is quite happy with the simple fare of grilled fish, steak sandwiches, and juicy burgers, as long as they are accompanied by Perry's trademark house-made potato chips. Others come just for the bar, known for its veteran bartenders who might look askance at those who order a silly drink like a cosmopolitan. Many of the people occupying the sports bar's stools look like they have been there for more than thirty years, but the neighborhood's well-informed youngsters are regular patrons as well. It's the kind of place that's cool enough to take a date, but sufficiently calm to please the folks when they visit from out of town. Open daily 9:00 A.M. to 11:00 P.M.; bar stays open until midnight. Call 922–9022.

Most of the shops on Union Street these days are of the elite variety—mostly high-class boutiques and designer eyewear studios—but there are a few for the rest of us. Those with kids shouldn't miss **Ambassador Toys** (1981 Union Street). A nice antidote to the big chain toy stores, Ambassador carries a range of playthings you won't find anywhere else, many of them handmade and bought from small suppliers around the world or at least on six continents. Little girls will particularly love the dress-up area upstairs, where they can try on princess and ballerina costumes. Open daily 10:00 A.M. to 7:00 P.M. Call 345–8697 or visit www.ambassadortoys.com.

The most eye-catching building in Cow Hollow is the **Vedanta Temple** (2963 Webster Street), which combines several different world styles on top of a typical San Francisco Edwardian. The 1905 building was built on an $1,800 sand lot as 'The First Hindu Temple in the Whole Western World' by the Vedanta Society of Northern California, followers of an ancient form of Hinduism that values the pursuit of knowledge. One of the tenets of Vedanta is that all religions are legitimate paths to understanding the spiritual world, and the eclectic style of the temple's roof is meant to reflect that view. Each of the five domes on the building's roof represents a different cultural and religious tradition, from the castle tower shape for Western Europe to the onion domes of the eastern tradition. Little seems to go on in the temple these days, and the real attraction is just gawking at its weirdness.

Six Gallery

North Beach is the neighborhood most associated with the beat writers, being home to the bars, cafes, and bookstores that they frequented, but Cow Hollow was the site of one of the movement's most important events. The building at 3119 Fillmore Street once housed the Six Gallery, where on October 13, 1955, many of the poets who would soon gain renown as the beats gathered to drink wine in bulk and read their verse. Lawrence Ferlinghetti, Jack Kerouac, Neal Cassidy, and poet-emcee Kenneth Rexroth were there, but the evening became historic when Allen Ginsberg took the stage to read his new poem, "Howl." Ginsberg's reading blew everyone away.

Kerouac immortalized the event in his novel *Dharma Bums,* changing a few names: "Everyone was there. It was a mad night. And I was the one who got things jumping by going around collecting dimes and quarters from the rather stiff audience standing around in the gallery and coming back with three huge gallon jugs of California Burgundy and getting them all piffed so that by eleven o'clock when Alvah Goldbrook was reading his wailing poem 'Wail' drunk with arms outspread everybody was yelling 'Go! Go! Go!' and old Rheinhold Cacoethes the father of the Frisco poetry scene was wiping tears in gladness."

Just up the waterfront from the perpetually tourist-choked Fisherman's Wharf area is the often neglected **Fort Mason.** This decommissioned army complex, set on a bluff overlooking the bay and a series of piers below it, combines beautiful open spaces, an important piece of American military history, and a local arts haven—all with some of the best views in the city.

Originally the site of an eighteenth-century Spanish gun battery, the United States Army seized the land from residents and mounted twelve cannons of its own here in 1864. These guns, along with others at Fort Point, Alcatraz, and Angel Island, were aimed to protect the Union bay during the Civil War. The fort saw no action during that faraway conflict, but was turned into the army's West Coast shipping center and served a major role as an embarkation point during World War II. Some 1.5 million troops shipped out from Fort Mason on their way to the Pacific theater. The fort was decommissioned after the Korean War and became part of the Golden Gate National Recreation Area.

Down a staircase from the bluff are the piers of Fort Mason Center (www.fortmason.org), a series of ugly buildings that in 1977 were turned into a haven for the city's arts and culture scene. Among the forty-some resident organizations in the five red-and-white former shipping depots, functionally called Buildings A through E, are the Museo Italo Americano (Building C, First Floor, 673–2200, www.museoitaloamericano.org); the San Francisco Museum of Modern Art Artists Gallery (Building A North, 441–4777, www.sfmoma.org); and Chinese Cultural Productions (Lily Cai Chinese Dance Company, Building C, Third Floor, Room 353, 474–4829, www.ccpsf.org).

Walk to the end of the piers for a fantastic view of the northern part of the bay and Alcatraz. The view is better than the one at nearby Pier 39, and instead of being surrounded by tourists, you will share the pier with Chinese fishermen casting for kingfish. Even on a sunny summer day, these guys will be wearing parkas and fur-lined hats, so bring a jacket.

Fort Mason also houses **Greens Restaurant,** the city's finest vegetarian establishment. Even those who can't conceive of a meal without meat are advised to experiment here, for the experience if not the cuisine. Greens lives in a massive shipping warehouse, but from the moment you pull open the black walnut doors, the utilitarian facade fades from memory. This is mostly because of the breathtaking view over the bobbing boats to the Golden Gate Bridge and the green hills of Marin County. Greens was founded by the San Francisco Zen Center, which seems to have created harmony in the building's interior. The airy space, with its 30-foot-high warehouse ceilings, is set off by the giant, twisting hunk of redwood tree near the entrance. From the stump of a tree cut down more than a hundred years ago, artists have made an inviting seating area, the only thing that competes with the view for your attention.

The menu changes nightly, but it is always filled with delicious, light items like tofu brochettes, white-corn griddle cakes, and wonderful soups and salads. Greens definitely has a gourmet reputation, but it is anything but stuffy, and the distracting view makes it a favorite for family gatherings. If you've got a party of about six, call ahead and ask for the private room with its own bay window. Open Monday through Saturday 5:30 to 9:00 P.M., Tuesday through Saturday noon to 4:00 P.M., Sunday 10:30 A.M. to 2:00 P.M. Call 771–6222. *Greens to Go* offers many of the same dishes for takeout Monday through Thursday 8:00 A.M. to 8:30 P.M., Friday and Saturday until 5:00 P.M., Sunday 9:00 A.M. to 4:30 P.M. Call 771–6330. Moderate.

Although once a pretty average working-class neighborhood on the relative outskirts of town, the *Marina District* is now the indigenous home of the San Francisco yuppie. After going off to college and finding temporary refuge in a fraternity or sorority house, this is where they return to, like the swallows to Capistrano. Not surprisingly then, the Marina is a beautifully maintained area, filled with nice bars and restaurants, though lacking much of an edge, especially since some of it was reconstructed after the 1989 Loma Prieta earthquake. The commercial center of the neighborhood is *Chestnut Street,* a lively strip that in recent years has seen chain businesses flood in and many of its interesting art deco facades covered over in the homogenization that inevitably follows. Locals may well be dismayed over the impending conversion of a classic movie house into a health club, but in this neighborhood, certainly, toned abs and glutes come first. Antiseptic though it may be, Chestnut is still a very nice street to stroll and offers some great "only in the Marina" shopping opportunities.

While the humans that populate the Marina District can intimidate, flaunting their designer sportswear and gym-toned physiques, it's the dogs that can really give you an inferiority complex. From the large ones with their aristocratic snouts to the little guys peeking their well-coiffed heads out of handbags, these canines are clearly living well, and they don't lack self-esteem. Few of the Marina's young professionals have kids, so they pamper the pets instead. Lest you doubt the veracity of this claim, poke your head inside *Catnip+bones* (2220 Chestnut Street). "A place for pets and their people," this is indeed a gourmet delicatessen and fashion boutique for the four-legged set. Does Fido look a little ragged in that sweater that grandma knitted? Just choose from the array of outerwear, including plaid flannel, brown corduroy, military fatigues, bright yellow rain slickers, and, naturally, sleek black leather. Concerned that his little head might get cold when the fog rolls in? Which goes better with his outfit: the Sam Spade fedora, the biker hat, or the tam o'shanter?

All right, so man's best friend might be a little bit humiliated by the prêt-à-porter, but he will certainly salivate over the cuisine. Among the doggie-safe tempting treats are bacon croissants, sushi cookies, lamb and turkey links, chur-ros, cream-filled cannoli, and peanut butter banana bonbons. And, in case he's got a date later, you can pick up a can of doggie breath mints. Some of the food looks like it could catch on with humans. It's not too hard to imagine a person splitting a bag of calamari jerky with his or her cat. And if leaving your pet alone fills you with guilt, the shop sells videotapes of birds and mice to entertain kitty, and stuffed dogs that grunt when squeezed. Open Monday through Saturday 10:00 A.M. to 8:00 P.M., Sunday 10:00 A.M. to 6:00 P.M. Call 359–9100.

No matter how yuppified the Marina gets, there will always be a place on Chestnut Street for *Lucca Delicatessen* (2120 Chestnut Street). This little fam-ily-owned shop has been serving up Italian meats, cheeses, coffees, cookies, and other food products since 1929, and if the Great Depression didn't sink them, neither will a change in neighborhood demographics. When the sun is out, make this your last stop before heading to the water's edge for an idyllic picnic. Open Monday through Friday 9:00 A.M. to 6:30 P.M., Saturday and Sun-day 9:00 A.M. to 6:00 P.M. Call 921–7873. Inexpensive.

The prime spot to engage in the Marina sports of seeing, being seen, using WiFi access, sipping European-sounding coffee, and showing off your new duds is *The Grove* (2250 Chestnut Street). While its clientele is often amusing, the place itself is quite charming, with its unfinished, knotty wood floors, wide bench seating, and a continuous stream of sultry blues pouring out of the stereo. Though housed in an old-time art deco building once common in the Marina, the decor inside is of the arts-and-crafts variety. The food is simple but tasty, consisting mainly of salads and hot and cold sandwiches. If you are lucky enough to snag one of the outside tables, you have scored the prime spot to watch the neighborhood go by. You can sit there as long as you want and make like a Marina-ite, but be sure to press a cell phone to your ear occasion-ally, lest the locals peg you as an outsider. Open daily 7:00 A.M. to 11:00 P.M. Call 474–4843. Inexpensive.

Marking the Marina District's western edge is one of San Francisco's most beloved buildings, the *Palace of Fine Arts* (3601 Lyon Street). You can't miss the salmon-colored Roman dome rising incongruously but grandly above the low-slung houses of the neighborhood. It should be noted right away that there is no fine art at the palace, at least not any more. Luckily, the beauty of the place and the immense pleasures to be had from wandering among its colon-nades and picnicking next to its duck-filled pond tend to temper the disap-pointment of uninformed tourists who come all the way from downtown expecting canvases and sculptures.

As it turns out, these art lovers have the right idea, they're just about ninety years late for the exhibition. The Palace of Fine Arts is the last remaining structure from the 1915 Panama Pacific International Exposition, when it played host to works from artists around the world. The 1915 fair was San Francisco's coming-out party, a chance to show the world, which had largely written the city off as a devastated wasteland, that it had recovered from the 1906 earthquake and fire and would be a major international city for years to come. The desire among prominent San Franciscans to show off the city's resilience dovetailed nicely with the opening of the Panama Canal in 1914. This bridging of the oceans revolutionized San Francisco's shipping industry, much as the transcontinental railroad had made overland travel to and from the east reasonable. There was no longer any need to send ships and their precious cargo on the harrowing trip around Cape Horn to reach San Francisco, and the city, still the biggest on the West Coast, gained a new prominence within the nation's economy.

To make room for the fair, engineers essentially produced a new patch of land, filling in the shallow lagoons that had lapped up against Cow Hollow and creating what would come to be known as the Marina District. The entire stretch of land from Fort Mason to the Palace of Fine Arts was occupied by the fair. Its attractions were housed in many other grand structures, with exhibits on agriculture, transportation, and metallurgy, to name a few.

The fair's buildings, as ambitious as they were, were designed to be temporary. Rather than spend the money erecting stone or wood structures that would probably be torn down for housing anyway, architects built them with chicken wire and plaster, making the whole production as easy to dismantle as papier-mâché. When the exposition closed in December 1915, the whole fair was to be razed, but the city had fallen in love with the stately Palace of Fine Arts, and a petition drive was started to save it. Luckily for the building, it was the only one of the fair's major structures that stood on military land, leaving its plot free of the ravenous appetites of developers, and the city decided to leave it in place. No one was quite sure what to do with it, however, and it served many prosaic uses over the following decades: a tennis court, a storage depot for army equipment, temporary fire department headquarters, and a distribution center for telephone books. As the years passed, the palace fell into disrepair, its temporary construction materials withering under the elements and heavy use. In the late 1950s, after a fund-raising drive led by a man named Walter Johnson, whose house looked out on the crumbling structure, the city tore the palace down to its metal frame and recast it in concrete, ensuring its endurance.

In the building behind the palace's rotunda is the ***Exploratorium*** (3601 Lyon Street), a museum of science aimed mostly at kids but popular with adults as well. The museum was founded in 1969 by Frank Oppenheimer, a physics professor whose brother Robert had led the team of scientists that developed the atomic bomb. As a counterpoint to the fear of science initiated by the atomic age, Oppenheimer had the idea of creating a place where ordinary people could be exposed firsthand to the magic and beauty of science. "The whole idea of the Exploratorium is to make it possible for people to believe they can understand the world around them," he wrote.

Oppenheimer's vision seems to have been realized, as on any given day the Exploratorium is packed with people fascinated by the roughly 400 hands-on exhibits on natural phenomena. Some demonstrations tease the viewer with optical illusions that persist even after they are explained. Others show the way light particles behave, how sound travels, or why an arched structure is so strong. One section of the museum that requires an advance reservation is the Tactile Dome, a maze of ladders, slides, and corridors that children must navigate in complete darkness (monitored on infrared cameras). Open Tuesday through Sunday 10:00 A.M. to 5:00 P.M. Admission is $10.00 for adults; $9.50 for students, children ages five to seventeen, and seniors; $8.00 for children ages four to twelve; and free for children younger than four. Admission is free the first Wednesday of the month. The Tactile Dome and Exploratorium combined admission is $15. Call 397–5673 or visit www.exploratorium.edu.

The Exploratorium does have one exhibit that is not inside the museum's walls, which is just as well because it has outgrown the Palace of Fine Arts site. Museum officials hope to relocate bayside and the search for space continues. Across Marina Boulevard from the museum, on a jetty next to the Marina Yacht Club, is the *Wave Organ,* a "sound sculpture" run by the tides. Local environmental artists installed pipes in the stone that lead down into the water. To experience the wave organ, put your ear up against a pipe's opening and listen to the strange sounds. The music can sometimes be disappointing; for the best results, go at high tide.

The heart of the *Presidio,* where most of the business took place during the area's days as a military garrison, is the *Main Post,* today the center of the Presidio's cultural mission. A good place to start your exploration is the *Visitor Information Center,* technically temporary but, a staffer says, permanent for the forseeable future, in the former Officers' Club (Building 50) on Moraga Avenue. The center offers piles of pamphlets, maps, and self-guided tour suggestions, and the enthusiastic volunteers and Golden Gate National Recreation Area staff can help too.

The visitor center also houses some memorabilia and a few exhibits on the Presidio's past. Ask if the scale model, behind glass, of the entire Marina District as it would have looked in 1915 during the Panama Pacific International Exposition, when the green-domed Horticulture Palace and the glittering Tower of Jewels beckoned visitors from around the world is available for

Great Views in the Presidio

The Presidio, with its prime location and hilly terrain, has a number of fantastic and thoughtful spots from which to admire the view. The recently remodeled Inspiration Point, a pull-off from Arguello Boulevard, provides a view over the top of some of the Presidio's lovely forests, a truly inspiring sight in the big city. This is also a jumping-off point for some nice walking trails through the city. A five-minute walk from the side of Washington Street takes you to the top corner of the San Francisco National Cemetery, set on a gently sloping hill. The towers of the Golden Gate Bridge rise behind the rows and rows of headstones. About a mile farther along Washington, before it meets Lincoln Way, is the World War II Memorial, carved with the names of 413 members of the armed forces lost or buried at sea in the Pacific. The memorial sits poignantly on a bluff above the ocean, providing excellent views of the setting sun.

public viewing. (Exhibits and their venues are changing frequently during reconstruction of many Presidio buildings.) If you have already spent some time walking the neighborhood's streets, little will look familiar except for the stately Palace of Fine Arts.

Many would-be artifacts are in storage waiting for an expansion and seismic retrofitting of Building 102, an old barracks building. If you're lucky, there will be a case of items from the Presidio's various areas that were found buried in the muck of Crissy Field during that area's rehabilitation. The mud preserved the pieces, including bottles, painted crockery, a hairbrush, and a polished bone toothbrush, quite nicely. The visitor center is open from 9:00 A.M. to 5:00 P.M. every day. Call 561–4323 or visit www.nps.gov/prsf or www.presidiotrust.gov.

Although the Presidio's soldiers never had to repel an enemy attack, their presence in the city proved critical in 1906, when the earthquake-caused fires ravaged San Francisco, and the fire department was badly understaffed. The soldiers helped fight the fire and maintain order in the devastated city. On the other side of the visitor center, behind the Old Post Hospital, are a pair of one-room wooden houses, painted green. These are two examples of the **Refugee Huts** that the army built and guarded for the thousands of families left homeless by the disaster. Huts much like these filled the city's parks in the months after the disaster, and once families found housing, many towed the huts into their yards, using them as tool sheds and the like or building around them in a way that left them unrecognizable. The owner of a house in the Sunset District found these two in her yard and donated them to the Presidio for use as a museum. One of the 10-by-30-foot shacks is hung with photos of the refugee camps and devastated regions of the city. The other has been appointed with period furniture and accoutrements to give some idea of what life in the camps would have been like. The simple bed, footlocker, and sink lend some verisimilitude, but the details—lace curtains, a stained plate and fork, and a cracked porcelain chamber pot—really bring you there. As horrible as life must have been, the huts now seem quite spacious and comfortable. On San Francisco's absurd real estate market, they'd be sure to fetch a high return. The huts are generally locked, leaving you to peer in the windows, but tours are offered occasionally by the National Park Service. Call 561–4323 for more information.

On a hill above the northwest corner of the Main Post, reached by a short walking trail from the end of Moraga Avenue, is the **Post Chapel.** Built in 1931, it houses some of the Presidio's most important art, both old and new. In a small room to the left of the main chapel is the Presidio Mural, a 34-foot-wide and 13-foot-high work depicting the history of the Presidio and California up to the 1930s. The mural, like so many of the city's other wonderful public art projects, was commissioned by the federal Works Progress Administration. Victor Mikhail Arnautoff, a Ukrainian expatriate who fought in the czar's army but fled during the Bolshevik revolution, got the commission. In addition to serving as technical director of the recently completed Coit Tower murals, Arnautoff was a graduate of the San Francisco Art Institute and had studied in Mexico with Diego Rivera.

Beginning in December 1934, Arnautoff and his assistants took forty-two days to complete the piece. The richly detailed mural is divided into three panels. On the left is a depiction of early Spanish and Russian settlers interacting with the native population. The center panel, focusing on religion, is dominated by a statue of St. Francis of Assisi with a view of downtown San Francisco and the bay behind him. If you turn around and look out the window, you will see that, although the statue does not exist, you are seeing the same view. The right side represents science and technology, with an image of the Panama Canal, so critical to San Francisco's development, and engineers studying the project for a bridge to span the Golden Gate.

Artistic activity at the chapel did not stop in the 1930s. In the late months of World War II, Army Chaplain Fredrick Alexander McDonald began collecting fragments of glass from the bombed-out churches of Europe and brought them back to the states. He carefully labeled them and put them in a box, where they stayed for fifty years. Upon hearing his story, local artist Armelle LaRoux decided to use the fragments to create new windows, which will eventually be installed at the chapel. Some of the completed works are in the chapel's basement. Call 561–3930 for hours and arrangements to see the windows.

A convenient amenity as you walk the often foggy and windy path toward the beckoning Golden Gate Bridge is the **Warming Hut** (983 Marine Drive), a cafe and gift shop run by the National Park Service. The prices are reasonable, and the food—sandwiches, pastries, and soups mostly—might be just what it takes to keep you going. In addition to the many books, posters, and items of apparel for sale, the Warming Hut also gives out free maps of the Presidio. Open daily from 9:00 A.M. to 5:00 P.M. Call 561–3042. Inexpensive.

From the Warming Hut, walk along the paved Golden Gate Promenade for about a half mile to reach ***Fort Point National Historic Site,*** the only Civil War–era fort on the West Coast. Soon after California's admission to the Union in 1850, leaders of the U.S. Army and Navy saw the need to defend San Francisco Bay and set about converting this jutting piece of land to military specifications. The plot was perfectly positioned to seal off access to the bay, but the problem was that it was set on a cliff. Because the military wanted a fort nearer to sea level so that cannons could fire balls that would skim the water and pierce enemy ships' hulls, they decided to dynamite the cliff from 90 feet to 15. The three-story fort was constructed with brick walls 7 feet thick, and in 1861 Col. Albert Sidney Johnson, commander of the Pacific fleet, mounted the first cannon and began moving in troops. A few months later, with the attack on the similarly constructed Fort Sumter in South Carolina, the Civil War began. Johnson, a Kentuckian, resigned his commission to join the Confederate Army. He died a year later in the battle of Shiloh.

Far away as it was from the theaters of battle, Fort Point never saw any action, its soldiers remaining on guard for an enemy that was otherwise occupied. According to some sources, a Confederate ship was on its way to attack

Fort Point and Golden Gate Bridge

Pet Cemetery

The Golden Gate National Recreation Area has taken great pains recently to restore wetlands in this part of the Presidio. Most people are grateful for the effort, but the Presidio's dog walkers are less pleased. As part of the restoration, the authorities have started enforcing a leash law, to keep man's best friend from chasing away the native birds. This is a big deal in the Presidio, because people here take their pets seriously. The best example of this is just a five-minute walk up McDowell Road from Crissy Field. For here, under the ominous rumble off the Golden Gate Bridge approach, lies the Presidio Pet Cemetery, final resting place for many of the decommissioned army base's beloved critters, where, even now, new unauthorized headstones appear. At first glance, the fenced-in area might seem like a joke, with its mostly particle-board headstones all slightly atilt. But further examination shows how serious it is. Among the more touching epitaphs is one that says, "Charlie was my favorite pet I every [sic] had. He was my bird 1976–1981." Some of the plots, which seem to be placed wherever there is room in a cemetery the National Park Service says is full, are more elaborate than others, such as the twin stone markers, each about 3 feet high, engraved with odes to a pair of late, lamented hounds, Mr. Twister and Raspberry. The latter's gravestone reads: "It's true my Basset has gone away, I know we had to part; But she'll be with me every day, within my loving heart."

San Francisco, but the war ended before it could complete the long journey. The fort is well preserved, although the view has changed dramatically. It is difficult to imagine the cannons loosing a charge today, because they might hit one of the towers of the Golden Gate Bridge, built right over the top of the fort in 1937, though occasional simulations directed by docents in uniform teach cannon crew teamwork and respect for what was the very real danger from explosive powder. A stairway leads up from here to the decks of the bridge, a walk of fifteen minutes or so, but Fort Point offers the unique view of the famous bridge's underside.

The troops have long since left Fort Point, leaving the really dangerous work to the surfers who ply the water around it. It's easy to see what makes this spot popular—notably the huge waves, long rides, and picturesque surroundings—but as you stand and watch the surfers hang ten, you'll probably wonder if they haven't lost their judgment after one too many wipeouts. The big breakers take the brave souls perilously close to the enormous boulders that line the point, and from time to time, as the water dips in one area to feed those enormous swells, a previously invisible rock will rear its head, making the danger even more apparent. These guys know what they're doing, using their familiarity with the current to steer just far enough from the rocks to be safe, but just close enough to wow the onlookers. And while the surf is certainly fantastic, there's also just something cool about riding the waves that break directly under the most famous bridge in the world. Open Friday through Sunday 10:00 A.M. to 5:00 P.M. The bridge, however, may be closed some days for retrofitting. Admission is free. Call 556–1693 or visit www.nps.gov/fopo.

Places to Stay in Cow Hollow, the Marina, and the Presidio

Edward II Inn & Suites
3155 Scott Street
922–3000
www.edwardii.com
Built to accommodate those attending the 1915 Panama-Pacific Exposition a few blocks away, the Edward II provides its modern guest choices of a queen bed with down-the-hall bathroom or a suite with a fireplace and Jacuzzi. Walk to the Presidio or jog along Marina Green a few blocks north. Moderate.

Hotel del Sol
3100 Webster Street
921–5500
www.jdvhospitality.com/hotels/hotel/5
Here, one of the Joie de Vivre boutique hotels is a 1950s-era motel with a central pool, saved from that time's unexciting design by bright, tropical colors in the green and orange reminiscent of yesteryear.

Hammocks and solicitous service give it distinction, while free parking (in San Francisco!) and breakfast by the pool seem deluxe. Moderate.

Union Street Inn
2229 Union Street
346–0424
www.unionstreetinn.com
This comfortable six-room bed-and-breakfast in a refurbished Edwardian house is right in the middle of Cow Hollow's shopping district. The inn has a pleasant garden where you can retreat for afternoon tea. Expensive.

Places to Eat in Cow Hollow, the Marina, and the Presidio

Liverpool Lil's
2942 Lyon Street
921–6664
At this British-style pub across the street from the Presidio's Lombard Gate, the

crowds are usually festive and the dishes hearty and meat-filled. Open Monday through Friday 11:00 to 1:00 A.M., Saturday and Sunday 10:00 A.M. to midnight. The bar is open until 1:00 A.M. every day. Moderate.

Rose's Cafe
2298 Union Street
775–2200
One of the more popular places on Union Street, Rose's tables are full at breakfast, lunch, and dinner. The dishes are mostly country Italian with an emphasis on seafood. Open Monday through Friday 7:00 A.M. to 10:00 P.M., Saturday and Sunday 8:00 A.M. to 11:00 P.M. Moderate.

The West Side

Sandwiched between San Francisco's two mammoth public lands, the Presidio and Golden Gate Park, the **Richmond District** often gets overlooked. Most who live in the eastern neighborhoods think of it as a boring bedroom community on the way to the parks or the beach. What they don't know is that this section of the city has its share of interesting shopping streets, good restaurants, and fun places to visit.

The most striking piece of architecture in the Richmond is **Temple Emanu-El** (2 Lake Street at Arguello Boulevard), a Byzantine structure that is home to San Francisco's biggest Jewish congregation, the oldest Jewish Congregation west of the Mississippi River. The 150-foot tan dome looms large over the two- and three-story houses that surround it, making it the area's primary landmark. You'll need a ticket to get a seat on Rosh Hashanah or Yom Kippur, but on an average Saturday morning you should have no problem. With its high Bavarian traditions, Emanu-El's services can be more austere than the typical Jewish service, a feeling accentuated by the music from the 4,500-pipe organ and the paid choir singing from a loft out of view. Call 751–2535 or visit www.emanuelsf.org. Muni Bus 33.

The rest of the Richmond's attractions are clustered at the area's far western end, about 3 miles from the Clement Street

THE WEST SIDE

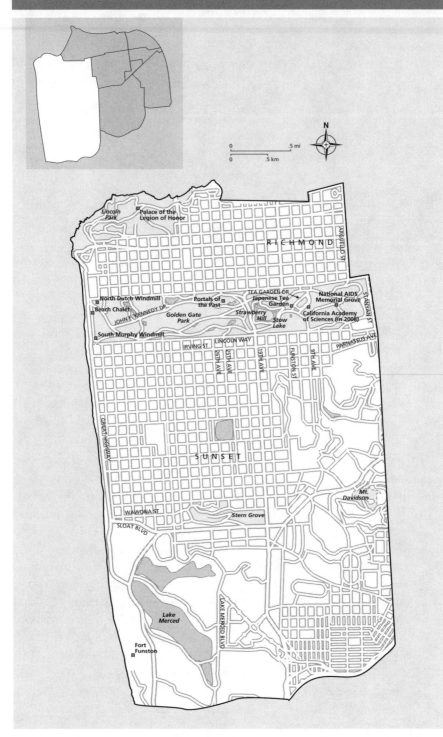

N

0   .5 mi
0   .5 km

Lincoln Park
Palace of the Legion of Honor

RICHMOND

ARGUELLO ST

North Dutch Windmill
Beach Chalet
JOHN F. KENNEDY DR
Golden Gate Park
South Murphy Windmill

Portals of the Past

TEA GARDEN OR Japanese Tea Garden
Strawberry Hill
Stow Lake

National AIDS Memorial Grove
California Academy of Sciences (in 2008)

ST ANSGAR ST
PARNASSUS AVE

IRVING ST
LINCOLN WAY
26TH AVE
25TH AVE
19TH AVE
FUNSTON ST
9TH AVE

GREAT HIGHWAY

SUNSET

Mt. Davidson

WAWONA ST
SLOAT BLVD

Stern Grove

Lake Merced
LAKE MERCED BLVD

Fort Funston

shopping district. If you are without a car, you'll need to grab a bus, probably the 2 or 38, to reach these spots.

Set gloriously on a cliff high above the ocean is **Lincoln Park,** most of which is given over to a public golf course. The green space also holds one of San Francisco's finest art museums, the grandiose **Palace of the Legion of Honor** (100 34th Avenue). Donated by one of the city's great philanthropists, Alma de Bretteville Spreckels (the same lady is *Victory,* atop Union Square's Dewey Monument) it is the permanent version of the temporary French Pavilion that stood in the Marina District during the 1915 Panama Pacific International Exposition. That building, designed as a replica of the Palais de la Légion d'Honneur in Paris, caught Spreckels's eye, and she commissioned a permanent version in the current spot. The advent of World War I put the project on hold, and when it was finally completed in 1924, Spreckels dedicated it to all of the Americans who died in the Great War. The museum has a vast collection of mostly European art and features touring exhibitions year-round, but the building itself, with Rodin's *The Thinker* in front of the main museum entrance, is the main draw. Open Tuesday through Saturday 9:30 A.M. to 5 P.M, Friday to 9:00 P.M. Admission is $8.00 for adults, $6.00 for seniors, $5.00 for ages twelve to seventeen, and free for children eleven and younger and for everyone on Tuesdays. Call 863–3330 or visit www.thinker.org/legion/index.asp.

Lincoln Park also has some of the finest views of the Golden Gate Bridge and the Pacific Ocean. Occupying one of these great ocean vistas, at a place called Point Lobos, is the **USS San Francisco Memorial.** The *San Francisco* took part in the World War II naval battle of Guadalcanal. Rather than an elegant statue, the memorial consists of a battered, bullet-ridden chunk of the ship's bridge. Inscribed next to it are the names of the 107 sailors lost in that two-day engagement. Twice a year, around Memorial Day and Pearl Harbor Day, those who survived the battle gather to remember those who weren't so lucky.

Now head out of the Lincoln Park area (follow Point Lobos Avenue) toward the ocean. Look just below the curving road, and you might rub your eyes at the sight of what appear to be ancient ruins. You are not gazing at the

TOP ATTRACTIONS ON THE WEST SIDE

Palace of the Legion of Honor	de Young Art Center
Sutro Baths	Mount Davidson
Golden Gate Park	

Palace of the Legion of Honor

remains of a Roman resort town, but at what is left of the **Sutro Baths,** a grand turn-of-the-twentieth-century swimming facility, museum, and amphitheater that burned down in 1966.

Adolph Sutro, a future mayor who at one time owned one-twelfth of San Francisco, opened the baths to the public in 1886. Visitors walked through a classical Greek portal into a hangarlike glass structure holding one freshwater pool, five saltwater pools ranging from cold to hot, and an enormous saltwater pool kept at ocean temperature. In all, the pools held 1,685,000 gallons of water and could be filled or emptied by the tides in an hour. The building also held three restaurants, a 3,700-seat amphitheater, and exhibits of artifacts from Aztec, Mexican, Egyptian, Syrian, and Japanese cultures. Sutro's endeavor was a hit, and San Franciscans streamed in, paying 25 cents to swim or 10 cents just to visit. By 1966, however, the baths were no longer profitable and the facility was sold to developers. A fire destroyed it soon after, leaving just the stone remains you see today. Many of the cultural exhibits are now held by San Francisco State University.

Walk down the hill to get a closer look at the baths. All that remains are pieces of stone foundation and the perimeter of one of the pools, which still fills up with ocean water. Even without the ruins, this is would be a lovely spot to admire the violent Pacific Ocean and the rocky coastline it has encouraged. To the right of the baths is a tunnel through the rocks where you can feel the surf thundering below your feet before you can see it through openings in the rocks. Be careful climbing around down here, though. The winds are often very high, and a sign advising of high surf includes the following admonishment: PEOPLE HAVE BEEN SWEPT FROM THE ROCKS AND DROWNED. Consider yourself warned.

When the powers-that-were of the growing city of San Francisco determined in the 1860s to build a large public park, they chose an unlikely swath of wind-blown sand dunes well beyond the developed areas. The city's leaders wanted an urban respite comparable to New York's Central Park. As it happened, the designer of that urban success story, Frederick Law Olmsted, had taken up residence in San Francisco, and he was the first choice to design the project. Olmsted, however, rejected the idea of trying to create a European-style park on such foreboding terrain, calling the idea wasteful and impossible. Instead he urged the city to build a smaller green consisting of native, drought-resistant plants on what is now Van Ness Avenue.

The city shrugged off Olmsted's concerns and hired a young engineer named William Hammond Hall to build *Golden Gate Park* (821–2700). Hall did some creative planting, using ice plants and European grasses known for their complex root systems to stabilize the sand, and employed a massive irrigation project to transform the land into a lush green space of 1,017 acres—larger than Central Park. Stretching from the Haight-Ashbury district in the east to Ocean Beach in the west, the area, with its many planned lakes and hills, quickly became a favorite destination for city dwellers and remains so today. Hall's design also dictated that all roads through the haven should be curved to slow the day's horse-drawn carriages. This trick still seems to work on today's vehicles, and many of the park's roads are closed to cars on weekends and holidays, leaving the roads to the many cyclists, skaters, skateboarders, joggers, and pedestrians. A free summer weekend and holiday shuttle program is also in place to move visitors around the vast area. Call 831–2727 for more information.

A good place to begin is in the *Beach Chalet* (1000 Great Highway), a 1925 Spanish Colonial Revival building on the park's western edge. The bottom floor is used for the *Golden Gate Park Visitor's Center,* which offers brochures for several of the area's attractions, schedules of guided tours, and historic exhibits, including a nifty scale model of the park. The room is also an attraction in itself, its walls covered with fresco murals and mosaics depicting 1930s life in San Francisco. During the Great Depression, the federal Works Progress Administration commissioned local artists to decorate the building, and the money was well spent. Muralist Lucien Labaudt created panels depicting people and neighborhoods around the city, including Fisherman's Wharf, Land's End, the Marina, Union Square, and Golden Gate Park itself. The detail

AUTHORS' FAVORITES ON THE WEST SIDE

Clement Street	Sushi at Ebisu
Sutro Baths	Fort Funston
Japanese Tea Garden	

is wonderful: The Golden Gate and Bay Bridges are depicted with only one tower each, as both were still under construction when Labaudt was drawing. The panel showing bathers enjoying Baker Beach includes a girl wearing a hat made of the newspaper's classified section. Among the advertisements visible are a 1936 Ford and a 1933 Lincoln for sale and an offer of help for "any girl in trouble or distress." This panel is where Labaudt depicted himself sitting on the beach with his back to the viewer; his wife and several of his design students mill about behind him. In the Fisherman's Wharf panel, Beach Chalet mosaicist Primo Caredio can be seen among the anglers repairing a fishing net, a cigarette dangling from his lips. Caredio's mosaics, made from designs conceived by Labaudt, are mostly complementary, with some very nice touches, including a Native American archer whose arrow points the way to the rest rooms. Above the doors on each side of the rectangular room, Labaudt added quotes from literature in reference to the wall's compass direction. On the western door, leading out to the beach, is a quote from Bret Harte: SERENE, INDIFFERENT OF FATE, THOU SITTEST AT THE WESTERN GATE.

If all the artwork has made you thirsty, fear not, for upstairs is the ***Beach Chalet Brewery & Restaurant,*** serving a variety of microbrews, housemade rootbeer, and soda and three meals a day with a fantastic view of the Pacific

Ocean. Even when the fog is so thick as to make the ocean all but disappear, the beer is still tasty, but choosing a sometimes rare sunny day is advisable. Open daily 9:00 A.M. to midnight, with live music Tuesday and Thursday through Saturday night. Call 386–4839 or visit www.beachchalet.com. The ***Park Chalet Garden Restaurant*** expands the space, with somewhat weather-protected views of the ocean. Pizza and barbeque are specialties. Moderate. Muni Metro N to Ocean Beach.

A five-minute walk down a dirt path behind the Beach Chalet takes you to the ***North*** (Dutch) ***Windmill,*** standing at 75 feet with four 102-foot arms, the windmill was built in 1903 to bring underground well water to the surface to be distributed to irrigate the park. Its career was short-lived, as in 1913 it was rendered obsolete by a more efficient system of motorized pumps. No

North (Dutch) Windmill

longer of any discernable use, it soon fell into disrepair and its spars stopped spinning. Strong winds subsequently tore the arms apart, and during World War II there was little reason to object to the military's commandeering of the metal parts. A restoration effort, completed in 1981, brought the windmill back, and further-needed restoration will be finished in 2006. The windmill looks its most picturesque, and most Dutch, in late winter (i.e., March to April) when the **Queen Wilhelmina Tulip Garden** comes to life. Some 10,000 bulbs are planted here each October and the colorful blooms flank the windmill beautifully.

The park's other turbine, the **South** (Murphy) **Windmill,** has recently been luckier. Located a fifteen-minute walk from the North Windmill, its canvas-covered spars have been replaced. Its cap was sent to Holland for authentic restoration. Complete, the South Windmill's spars will spin again in June 2005.

A trip of about two-thirds of a mile east on John F. Kennedy Drive takes you from the Netherlands to the Great Plains as you stumble upon the **Buffalo Paddock.** The awkward-looking beasts have been part of the park since 1892, when naturalists brought one male and one female, named Ben Harrison and Madame Sandra Bernhardt, from the plains of Kansas and Wyoming. The idea was to breed the creatures in captivity because they were threatened with extinction in the wild. With successful breeding and the addition of three brought in from Yellowstone Park, the paddock was home to thirty bison by 1918. Things went smoothly for the herd until 1980, when seven were diagnosed with bovine tuberculosis and removed from the paddock. Most of the bison you see today are descendants of a newer herd, donated in 1984 by Richard Blum, husband of then mayor and current United States Senator Dianne Feinstein. In 1993, a group of Lakota Sioux tribesmen from Wyoming came to Golden Gate Park to conduct a ceremony and give the bison Sioux names.

Two of the park's ten lakes are also worth a stop. **Lloyd Lake** sits near the middle of the park, along John F. Kennedy Drive, and on its northern shore is a lonely marble-and-brick portico. This entryway, now called **Portals of the Past,** once led into the Nob Hill mansion of A. N. Towne, vice president of the Southern Pacific Railroad. The mansion was completely destroyed in the earthquake and resulting fire of 1906, leaving only the entryway intact. The 10-foot-high marble columns hold up a mantel of brick. A few hundred feet up JFK Drive is **Stow Lake,** a small body of water surrounding Strawberry Hill. A twenty-minute climb up the hill leads to 360-degree views of the Sunset District and the Pacific Ocean beyond.

A right turn onto Hagiwara Tea Garden Drive leads to the **Japanese Tea Garden.** As you might expect from the name, the four-acre garden consists of pleasant paths through neatly manicured flower beds, with tea service provided by women in kimonos. While parents are leisurely sipping their tea, children will enjoy roaming the enclosed gardens and clambering over the ladderlike drum bridge, which rises like a camel's hump over a small stream. Other highlights include a bronze Buddha cast in Tajima, Japan, in 1790 and the Lantern of Peace, donated in 1953 by Japanese children as a symbol of friendship with the United States.

The immaculately maintained garden also carries a tragic story of a dark time in United States history. Makoto Hagiwara, an immigrant from Japan, designed the garden for the 1894 Midwinter Exposition that was the park's coming-out party. The exposition's creators wanted a mock Japanese village, but Hagiwara came up with the idea to make it a garden and to serve green tea, then unknown in North America. In 1914, Hagiwara also began serving a strange cookie folded around a piece of paper printed with a message. While fortune cookies are now mostly associated with Chinese restaurants, Hagiwara has been credited as their inventor. After the exposition ended, Hagiwara leased the garden from the city, and he and his family lived there and tended the garden. After Hagiwara's death in 1925, his daughter Tanako ran the garden with her children and grandchildren until the bombing of Pearl Harbor changed the lives of all Japanese-Americans. The Hagiwaras were forced to move to an internment camp in Utah, the name was changed to the Oriental Tea Garden, and the garden's care was given over to white San Franciscans. In 1986 the Recreation and Park Department changed the name of the street in front to "Hagiwara Tea Garden Drive" to honor the family, but the Hagiwaras were never again involved with the garden. Open daily from 9:00 A.M. to 6:00 P.M. March through September, and to 5:00 P.M. October through February. Admission is $3.50 for adults, $1.25 for seniors and children ages six to twelve. Call 752–4227. Muni Bus 44.

In front of the Tea Garden is the ***Music Concourse,*** where the Golden Gate Park Band, the oldest continually operating municipal band in the country, plays everything from classical to marches on Sunday afternoons in the summer. The music concourse, like the Tea Garden, is a remnant of the California International Midwinter Exposition of 1894. The fair, meant to emulate Chicago's Columbian Exposition of the previous year, was the brainchild of M. H. de Young, publisher of the *San Francisco Chronicle,* in whose pages, naturally, it was called "one of the greatest expositions the world has ever known." The one hundred temporary buildings erected for the fair, including the 266-foot Tower of Electricity, required the removal of 180 acres of trees, despite the protests of the park's superintendent, John McLaren. Although de Young claimed to be doing it all for the prestige of the city, he may have also been influenced by other factors. The owner of a good deal of the as yet undeveloped land surrounding the park, de Young certainly saw a few financial benefits in attracting people to the western part of the city.

The Music Concourse area and two of the three attractions around it— *de Young Museum* and *California Academy of Sciences*—are in a state of improvement and, in the case of the museums, being rebuilt. The concourse itself will have a parking lot underneath it (unless a legal decision ensues and stipulates otherwise). The band shell at the western end of the concourse will likely remain. The de Young Museum, famous for collections of textiles, artifacts from Africa and Oceania (such as indigenous art and objects from the South Pacific), and American art, was damaged in the 1989 Loma Prieta earthquake. Because of seismic concerns, the museum was unable to get insurance to host the traveling blockbuster exhibitions on which it and its sister fine arts museum, the Legion of Honor, depend. The de Young is starting from scratch on a site it had occupied for a century. When it opens in summer 2005, it will have a copper-colored skin designed to filter subdued light within and entrances from every direction. Visit www.thinker.org.

In 2008 the California Academy of Sciences, the city's natural history museum, is expected to move from its temporary South of Market (SOMA) location at 875 Howard Street back to a new, grass-covered-roof facility on its previous site across the Concourse from the Japanese Tea Garden and the de Young Museum. (See SOMA, p. 124 for information on its downtown operations, call 750–7145, or check the latest on exhibits at www.calacademy.org.)

The Academy of Sciences also sponsors the annual Run to the Far Side on Thanksgiving weekend. The 10K run through the park attracts some serious runners and some who run around dressed like Gary Larson creations. Why? The Academy of Sciences has housed a Gary Larson Gallery, a room filled with the best animal cartoons from Larson's hilariously zany "The Far Side." Some of the cartoons are used to teach science. One panel, depicting a parade of lemmings marching into the sea while one lemming, wearing a life preserver, smirks at the viewer, is used to make the point that lemmings don't actually intend to commit suicide. They set out because of overpopulation and "some dispersing individuals have a better chance of survival than others."

Behind the Academy of Sciences area is the *National AIDS Memorial Grove,* built in 1991 as a place for reflection on the victims of the disease that has particularly devastated San Francisco. Now a gorgeous 7.5-acre stretch of pathways in one of the park's valleys, it is hard to believe that this part of the park was previously a neglected sewage dump. The grove, named a national memorial in 1996, is now one of the most attractive areas in the park. It contains poignant reminders of the disease, like the Circle of Friends, a stone platform with the names of AIDS victims carved in concentric circles. Call (888) 294–7683 or 750–8340 or visit www.aidsmemorial.org.

One park rebuilding project is complete, the **Conservatory of Flowers.** The white-glass greenhouse, said to resemble the one in England's Kew Gardens, was built in the park in 1879. After a 1995 windstorm blew out many of the 10,800 whitewashed panes of glass from one hundred wooden arches and made structural stability questionable, an eight-year restoration made it shimmer again with state-of-the-art structural reinforcement and unbroken glass. One philodendron plant from Brazil is so old—a centenarian—that when the building was dismantled, the Conservatory ended up being rebuilt around the twining light-seeker. For a city with a touted Mediterranean climate with microclimates at every turn, the tropical rarities and huge specimens are the Bay Area's best introduction to jungle plants and the humidity they require. Don't miss the 6-foot-wide Amazon River water lilies in the aquatic garden. Open Tuesday through Sunday 9:00 A.M. to 4:30 P.M. Admission is $5.00 for adults, $3.00 for seniors and children ages twelve to seventeen, and $1.50 for children ages five to eleven. Call 666–7001 or visit www.conservatoryofflow ers.org for information.

South of Golden Gate Park lies the **Sunset District,** a mostly residential patch in the southwest corner of the city. Most San Franciscans devote little thought to the Sunset; one reason is the dense fog that occludes the sun on most days. Through a geological quirk, even when the rest of the city is basking in glorious sunshine, the Sunset is often socked in. This reputation renders the area undervisited and has led to the chestnut that the depressive effects of the fog make the Sunset the city's suicide capital. True or not, this part of the city boasts some nice sights and neighborhoods. Although it does not offer much in the way of quality lodging, it is easily reached by public transportation, and when the miasma lifts, the sunsets are indeed gorgeous.

Perhaps the most significant artwork in the Sunset is hidden away in a lecture room in the University of California San Francisco (UCSF) medical school's **Toland Hall** (533 Parnassus Avenue). To gaze at the ugly institutional high-rise you would never guess that the walls of its main lecture hall are covered with vibrant frescoes. In 1936 the university commissioned Bernard Zakheim, a Polish immigrant who studied with the great Diego Rivera, to decorate the room with murals that would depict the history of medicine in California. If the school had wanted an antiseptic view of the subject, however, it must have been disappointed. Zakheim's murals show with brutal honesty the realities of medicine's more ignorant moments, including the use of leeches and bleeding, and some of its great failures, as shown by the rat-infested corpses of Chinese laborers killed during an outbreak of bubonic plague. Panels showing Catholic missionaries

Civil War, San Francisco Style

Among its other unique traits, San Francisco has the dubious distinction of hosting the only duel ever to result in the death of a sitting United States senator. Add to this that the fatal shot was fired by the chief justice of California, and modern-day politics look polite in comparison.

David Broderick, a New Yorker, came to San Francisco during the Gold Rush of 1849, made a fortune in real estate, and gained a U.S. Senate seat as a Democrat in 1857. His abolitionist views made him a target among some of San Francisco's powerful people, including the state's top judge, David Terry. After Terry criticized him, Broderick called Terry a "miserable wretch." These were apparently fighting words, and Broderick accepted Terry's challenge to duel a few months later.

The two prominent men met on an early morning next to Lake Merced in the southwestern part of the Sunset District. Legend has it that Broderick's gun discharged before he aimed it, leaving him wide open for Terry's shot to his chest. After being hit, Broderick was rushed to his friend's house in what is now Fort Mason, where he died. Monuments mark the spots where Broderick and Terry each stood, in a park to the east of Lake Merced Boulevard. A sign along the road points the way.

mistreating Native Americans also generated controversy, especially since a local church had agreed to fund the frescoes. In 1948 one of the university's professors complained that the murals were too distracting to students and had them covered with wallpaper and shellac. As a final indignity, nails were driven into the walls to hang pictures of professors. Artist groups complained, and in 1962 the murals were uncovered. They were half destroyed, but Zakheim's son was able to restore them using his father's original sketches. Open when class is not in session. Call UCSF information at 476–9000 or 353–4436.

On Lincoln Way, which forms the southern border of Golden Gate Park, sits a pub called the **Little Shamrock** (807 Lincoln Way). Still a pleasant watering hole and a great place to throw darts or play backgammon, it was one of the neighborhood's first buildings. During the preparation of the park for the Midwinter Exposition, what is now the Sunset District was an uninhabited, sandy wasteland. With no residents in the area, it follows that there would be no pub, but the mostly Irish laborers who came out each day to build the park created a business opportunity. The men were working up quite a thirst, it seems, and had nowhere to slake it. Once the pub opened in 1893, it quickly gained popularity among the workers, offering a free lunch with a schooner of beer. Owner Tony Herzo even developed a service to carry shots of whiskey out to the workers on cold, foggy days.

The location was also a natural because, in the days before the streets were laid, a streetcar ran along what is now Lincoln Way all the way to Ocean Beach. The spot where the Little Shamrock sits was one of the train's two stops, and it was usually a long one as sand was cleared from the track farther down the line. The pub is still a great way station for enjoying a pint and gazing at the many historical artifacts on the walls. Among them is a clock that stopped at 5:13 A.M. on the day of the 1906 earthquake. The Little Shamrock survived the quake intact, but Jim O'Connor's pub next door was not so lucky, and he donated the clock after closing for good. After the disaster, when the park became an encampment, the Shamrock was once again an invaluable resource, serving free lunches to the newly homeless. Today the food is mostly limited to potato chips to accompany the thick stout. Open Monday through Thursday 3:00 P.M. to 2:00 A.M., Friday 2:00 P.M. to 2:00 A.M., Saturday and Sunday 1:00 P.M. to 2:00 A.M. Call 661–0060. Inexpensive. Muni Buses 44 and 71.

For a more highbrow experience, stop in the **Canvas Cafe and Gallery** (1200 Ninth Avenue at Lincoln Way). The cafe serves simple but upscale sandwiches, pizzas on focaccia, and salads, plus several beers on tap and in bottles. What makes the place unique is that while one end is full of tables, usually filled by cramming students from the nearby University of California Medical School, the other is a gallery for paintings and sculpture by little-known local artists. Open Sunday through Thursday 8:00 A.M. to midnight, Friday and Saturday to 2:00 A.M. Call 504–0060. Inexpensive.

Also on the first block of Ninth Avenue is **Le Video** (1231 Ninth Avenue), universally regarded as the best movie rental shop in San Francisco. The store is a favorite for its extensive selection of small independent films, subsections like '80s Teen Classics and Comic Book Heroes, and no less than eight shelves full of Alfred Hitchcock creations. What really sets it apart is its massive collection of foreign films. This section, which takes up most of the first floor, is alphabetized by country, and just about the entire United Nations is represented. Conveniently, the floor is marked with the countries' flags to make it easier to find the latest cinema from Zimbabwe or the Republic of Georgia. Customers are urged to visit the Web site (www.levideo.com) and to print out a floor plan in advance to aid navigation through the store. Open daily 10:00 A.M. to 11:00 P.M. Call 566–3606.

If visiting the Japanese Tea Garden and the aquarium has put you in mind of sushi, now might be a good time to pop into into **Ebisu** (1283 Ninth Avenue), just a few more steps down the street, one of the city's finest spots for raw fish. As you enter, the staff will make you feel at home with a hearty *irasshaimase* (welcome) and a warm towel. You can sit at a table with chairs or one with traditional tatami mats, but for the best experience sit at the counter, where the friendly chefs will prepare your maki rolls and nigiri (fish on a block of rice) to your order and scoop them directly onto your wooden plate. Ebisu and its sister restaurant across the street, *Hotei,* are named for two of the seven *shichifuku-jin,* or deities of good fortune, in Japanese culture. Ebisu traditionally represents success for fishermen, while Hotei is said to bring more general prosperity. Hotei also serves sushi from Ebisu but emphasizes noodle dishes. Ebisu is open daily 11:00 A.M. to 2:00 P.M. and 5:00 to 10:00 P.M. Call 566–1770. Moderate. Hotei is open every day but Tuesday 11:30 A.M. to 10:00 P.M. Call 753–6045. Moderate.

Walk a few steps to the south and you'll hit Irving Street, the main drag of what is known as the Inner Sunset. Muni Metro's N-Judah rumbles by this corner, and passengers disembark to do their shopping or lounge at the many cafes. The modern *Black Oak Books* (630 Irving Street; 564–0877, www.black oakbooks.com) on the northern side, has an excellent selection of new and used books. Open daily 10:00 A.M. to 10:00 P.M.

The best place in the neighborhood to feed your caffeine demons is *The Beanery* (1307 Ninth Avenue). While sipping a cup of rich organic brew, you can sit and watch the shop's roasting machine, named "The San Franciscan," churn through a selection of beans, including Sumatra Mandheling, Ethiopian

How Much Is That Doggie on the Rooftop?

Way out at the end of Sloat Boulevard, where the L-Taraval streetcar turns around and the smells of the beach make themselves known, looms an unlikely San Francisco landmark. The 7-foot-tall, 700-pound fiberglass head of a dachshund, with a chef's hat perched above its floppy brown ears and polka-dotted bow tie around its neck, was the symbol of the now defunct chain of Doggie Diner restaurants. Opened in 1949, Doggie Diner became a local institution in the 1960s and 1970s, with locations around the Bay Area. Opinions differ as to whether the food was any good, but consensus has it that the doggie heads were what really brought in the customers.

The restaurant began to struggle in the 1980s, and after it went out of business in 1986, the dog heads that peered proudly from the roofs started to disappear as well. The last holdout was the head that stood above the unremarkable Carousel Restaurant on Sloat Boulevard. When the new owners of the property announced plans to remove it, a public outcry ensued, and the board of supervisors worked out a plan for the city to take control of the head in 2000. The head was not safe yet. On April 1, 2001, high winds knocked the poorly maintained doggie off its perch, and it crashed into a phone booth below, crushing the nose. A fund-raising effort was quickly mounted, with the city putting up half the money, and after several literal ups and downs, the newly restored head is back on the roof looking goofy as ever, a monument to San Francisco kitsch.

Harrar, and Organic Guatemala Antigua. The Beanery's other location, around the corner on Irving Street, also offers tasty coffee but lacks the mesmerizing roaster. Light fare—bagels and pastries—is also available. Call 661–1255. Open Monday through Saturday 6:00 A.M. to 7:00 P.M. and Sunday 7:00 A.M. to 7:00 P.M. Inexpensive.

sterngrove

One of the Sunset's secrets is **Stern Grove,** a sliver of park land jammed into a canyon between Wawona Street and Sloat Boulevard. The area itself is pleasant enough, with grassy fields and a small lake hemmed in by eucalyptus trees, but in the summer it becomes a major neighborhood cultural attraction. Since 1938, orchestras and bands have played free Sunday concerts in this natural amphitheater, opera singers have trilled, and the San Francisco Ballet has danced. Thousands of people bring their lunches. Call 252–6252 for concert schedules, consult www.sterngrove.org, and, from mid-June to mid-August, call 831–5500 to reserve a limited number of picnic tables for the following week's concert.

Traveling west on Irving, the neighborhood becomes less yuppie and more Chinese. The part of Irving around 25th Avenue is known as the city's "Third Chinatown," and the shops offer many of the same items as in the original downtown. Other Asian groups have also staked a claim to this area, and several Japanese and Thai restaurants line the streets. Come to this neighborhood at mealtime and grab a table at **Marnee Thai** (2225 Irving Street). The small restaurant is considered by many one of the best Thai restaurants in the city, and it lives up to its billing. Particularly tasty are the noodle dishes, especially the melt-in-your-mouth pad se-ew (flat noodles fried with egg, broccoli, and your choice of meat) and koong sarong (prawns wrapped in bacon and a thin rice flour crepe). The walls and peaked ceiling of woven bamboo strips add to the experience nicely. Open daily from 11:30 A.M. to 10:00 P.M. Call 665–9500. Inexpensive. Muni Metro N-Judah, Bus 16 or 71.

Unlike the old Chinatown, where specialty shops sell various food products to shoppers, out in "The Avenues," all of a Chinese mother's shopping can be done at one store: **Sunset Supermarket** (2425 Irving Street). The building is laid out just like a typical supermarket, but with almost none of the same products. You can't beat the selection for Chinese food products, though. With fifteen kinds of dried shredded pork, jellyfish strips for $2.29 a pound, and live geoduck clams—with shells the size of Nerf footballs and brown protrusions as long as a toddler's arm—how can you go wrong?

As if to show that this neighborhood remains ethnically mixed, next door is **Tel-Aviv Strictly Kosher Meats,** owned by a Jewish immigrant from

Odessa, Russia (2495 Irving Street; 661–7588). Open Sunday through Tuesday and Friday, 8:00 A.M. to 6:00 P.M., Wednesday and Thursday 8:00 A.M. to 7:00 P.M., closed Saturday.

A hidden treasure in this neighborhood is the ***de Young Art Center*** (2501 Irving Street), a teaching facility for children on the corner of Irving Street and 26th Avenue. The art center had to leave the de Young museum building when it closed for renovations, so it has taken up residence on Irving Street until the museum reopens in 2005. The center offers free art workshops for children, many of them on a drop-in basis, and also hosts a different resident artist each month. The artist's work is displayed in the center, and he or she takes part in teaching the children. The center is open Tuesday through Friday 10:00 A.M. to 4:45 P.M., Saturday 1:00 to 5:00 P.M. Call 682–2485 or visit www.thinker.org for the month's schedule.

Perched proudly on the cliffs of San Francisco's southwest corner, ***Fort Funston*** (located off Skyline Boulevard) was a launching site for Nike missiles after World War II but is now known for the more peaceful launching of hang gliders. The fort's dramatic vantage point over the ocean that made it an ideal military stronghold also makes it the best place to watch humans propel themselves high into the air. The fort consists not so much of buildings, but of sandy walkways surrounded by various shrubs. A wooden observation deck has been conveniently placed for optimal ocean gazing. Besides hang gliding, the main activity at Fort Funston is dog walking. The walkers have proved a strong lobby to oppose the National Park Service's plan to establish parts of the fort as nature preserves, making them off-limits to dogs. Current regulations require that dogs be on leashes. Dogs and walkers alike need to be careful next to the open cliffs, however. Signs warn that people and dogs have been swept over the edge, and drawings depict one of each tumbling head over heels. Fort Funston is a good starting point for a walk along the coast in either direction. Open daily 10:00 A.M. to sunset. Call 561–4700 or 239–2366. Muni Bus 18.

anothercross to bear

Despite the stink that was raised about the Mount Davidson Cross, another cross on city land has been less controversial. *Prayerbook Cross,* a 75-foot structure made of sandstone, stands peacefully on a hill just off John F. Kennedy Drive in Golden Gate Park. The cross, well hidden by the park's trees, commemorates the first use of the Common Book of Prayer in California in a service aboard the ship of Sir Francis Drake in 1579. It should also be noted that although Drake sailed right past the Golden Gate and welcoming waters of San Francisco Bay, he never noticed it.

As the highest point in San Francisco, ***Mount Davidson*** (938 feet) is hard to miss. In recent years, however, the hill has gotten more attention because of a political and legal battle over it. The 103-foot concrete cross that towers at its peak prompted a court battle testing the doctrine of separation of church and state. Local residents, concerned over the propriety of such an enormous religious symbol planted prominently on city land, raised a stink. The city, reluctant to tear the cross down but eager to relinquish control, put the land up for auction in 1997, eventually selling it to the Armenian American Organizations of Northern California as a memorial to the Armenian genocide in Turkey. Complaints continued, particularly from local and national atheist groups, that the city was pulling a fast one with the Constitution, but a United States District Court judge ruled the sale legal, and the symbol still stands.

The city has taken pains to assure anyone who visits the peak that it is privately owned, with several signs at each approach explaining the city's belief in separation of church and state. The current cross, completed in 1934, is actually the fourth one to grace the pretty peak, the first three having burned down. President Franklin D. Roosevelt fired up the lights by telegraph from Washington, D.C., at the dedication ceremony. The cross is traditionally the site for an Easter sunrise service that was once an annual event on national television. To reach the cross, you must take a short but pleasant hike uphill through eucalyptus trees, and you can stop for a magnificent view of the southeastern part of the city.

Places to Stay on the West Side

Day's Inn
2600 Sloat Boulevard
665–9000
This branch of the national chain has newly remodeled rooms and, while far from elegant, is reasonably comfortable. It is across the street from the San Francisco Zoo and three blocks from the beach. Muni Metro L-Taraval. Inexpensive.

Great Highway Inn
1234 Great Highway
731–6644
www.greathwy.com
This massive, sprawling structure with clean, functional rooms is a two-minute walk from Ocean Beach, Golden Gate Park, and a streetcar line. Muni Metro N-Judah. Moderate.

Seal Rock Inn
545 Point Lobos Avenue
752–8000
www.sealrockinn.com
This family-owned hotel boasts large rooms, each with extraordinary views of the ocean. Muni Buses 18, 38. Moderate.

Places to Eat on the West Side

Bella
3854 Geary Boulevard
221–0305
People who love this trattoria have to be glad that it is out in the Richmond District, where people from the cooler neighborhoods can't find it. Its food is so good that, were it more centrally located, getting seated at one of the few tables would be nearly impossible. Those in the

know are treated to perhaps the best pasta dishes in the city. If you can get over the guilt, don't miss the fettuccine with rabbit sauce. Open Monday through Friday 11:30 A.M. to 3:00 P.M., Sunday through Thursday 5:30 to 9:30 P.M., Friday and Saturday to 10:30 P.M. Muni Bus 38. Moderate.

Eight Immortals

1433 Taraval Street
731–5515

The Bay Area Chinese community routinely packs this nondescript Parkside restaurant. Get there before 6:00 P.M., or earlier on weekends, when no reservations are accepted, for succulent garlicky greens and cooked-to-perfection fish specialties including shrimp, cod, and crab. Open Thursday through Tuesday 11:00 A.M. to 9:30 P.M. Moderate.

Java Beach

1396 La Playa Street
665–5282

This simple cafe offers basic sandwiches, salads, and traditional Irish breakfasts, and the hot coffee is a godsend on a typically foggy day at the beach. Open Sunday 6:00 A.M. to 9:00 P.M., Friday and Saturday until 10:00 P.M., Monday, Tuesday, and Thursday 5:30 to 9:00 P.M., Wednesday (Comedy Night) to 10:00 P.M. Inexpensive.

Marco Polo

1447 Taraval Street
731–2833

The sign also says "ITALIAN ICE CREAM" but this Chinese ice creamery, with its sad fluorescent lighting, serves something between gelato and ice cream. Neighborhood teenagers and couples, mostly Asian, flock here. Try red bean, durian (warning—smelly!), lychee, coconut, soursop, guava, mango, sesame, or a more Western rum raisin, vanilla, or black walnut. Open daily noon to 10:00 P.M. Inexpensive.

Park Chow

1240 Ninth Avenue
665–9912

Part pub, part family-style restaurant, Park Chow is one of the most popular spots in the Inner Sunset, serving Italian and Asian dishes along with fresh seafood. The excellent beer selection and irresistible dessert menu make this a hard restaurant to leave. Open Sunday 10:00 A.M. to 10:00 P.M., Monday through Thursday 11:00 A.M. to 10:00 P.M., Friday 11:00 A.M. to 11:00 P.M., Saturday 10:00 A.M. to 11:00 P.M. Muni Metro N to Eighth Avenue. Moderate.

Pluto's

627 Irving Steet
753–8867

With cafeteria-style dining at its most elegant, Pluto's "Fresh Food for a Hungry Universe" offers freshly grilled steak, roasted poultry, hearty vegetable side dishes, and made-to-order salads. There may be no better place for a quick, tasty meal. Open daily from 11:00 A.M. to 11:00 P.M. Muni Metro N to Eighth Avenue. Inexpensive.

The Central Neighborhoods

At San Francisco's center are several interesting neighborhoods that in many ways go together, but in other ways do not. For the purposes of this book, they are all included in this chapter and can be visited consecutively—via short bus rides or a long walk—or in separate trips.

Before 1967, the area just off the eastern edge of Golden Gate Park, around where Haight and Ashbury Streets collided, was not very notable even within San Francisco. It was essentially a working-class neighborhood with lots of Victorian houses that had seen better days. In the late 1960s, however, the big houses and cheap rents began to attract kids who were coming to San Francisco to be a part of the peace movement, the drug scene, and the famous free love. The **Haight-Ashbury** quickly became synonymous with these phenomena worldwide, and for a short time it was truly the place to be. Bands like the Grateful Dead, Jefferson Airplane, and Janis Joplin's Big Brother and the Holding Company were making it big from their houses in the neighborhood, while be-ins and other happenings were held in Golden Gate Park, and a general libertine spirit ruled the section. But signs of a crash abounded: The Hell's Angels had their headquarters in the supposedly peaceful Haight-Ashbury and had several run-ins with local police,

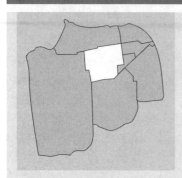

N

0 .25 mi
0 .25 km

BROADWAY

GOUGH ST

PACIFIC AVE

**PACIFIC
HEIGHTS**

Alta Plaza
Park

VAN NESS AVE

DIVISADERO ST

FILLMORE ST

CALIFORNIA ST

ARGUELLO ST

PINE ST

BUSH ST

SUTTER ST

Japan
Center

POST ST

GEARY BLVD

**WESTERN
ADDITION**

LORAINE CT

LAGUNA ST

MASONIC AVE

CENTRAL AVE

FULTON ST

SCOTT ST

**ALAMO
SQUARE**

FELL ST

Panhandle

OAK ST

PAGE ST

**HAIGHT
ASHBURY**

HAIGHT ST

Buena
Vista
Park

STANYAN ST

COLE ST

ASHBURY ST

14TH ST

presaging their role in the disastrous Rolling Stones concert in nearby Altamont in 1970. As seems inevitable today, by the end of the '60s the idealism had mostly faded, and the neighborhood took on a grungy, drug-ridden air that it is only now beginning to shake.

Walk down Haight Street today and you will almost certainly be harassed by so-called anarchists and offered drugs multiple times. That being said, there are stops, old and new, that still make a visit to Haight Street worthwhile. One of the street's modern treasures sits conveniently near the street's western end, just on the edge of the weirdness beyond. *Amoeba Music* (1855 Haight Street), which *Rolling Stone* magazine once called the best record store in the world, set up shop in the cavernous hull of an old bowling alley, and the click-clicking of hundreds of customers riffling through racks of compact discs echoes through the building the way clattering pins once did. The hip, the square, and everyone in between can be found scouring the equally extensive rock, dance, country, and classical sections, to name a few. The 25,000-square-foot store holds 400,000 CDs and 100,000 records, many of which reside in specialized categories, including Central Asian, Black Metal, and Unusually Experimental. An offshoot of a Berkeley store, Amoeba holds fast to that town's activist sensibilities. The store donates part of its proceeds to preserve rain forest land, claiming to have helped save one million acres so far. Amoeba also hosts free performances by local and touring bands several times a week. Call 831–1200 or visit www.amoebamusic.com/shows.html for performance schedules. The store is open Monday through Saturday from 10:30 A.M. to 10:00 P.M. and Sunday from 11:00 A.M. to 9:00 P.M.

The summer of love is over, but don't tell that to Sami Sunchild, owner of *The Red Victorian Bed, Breakfast, and Art* (1655 Haight Street) just up the street. Since the '60s, her inn has been putting up flower children and those sorry they missed the Haight's heyday, and she has not abandoned the ethic of peace and love. The Red Victorian, which is, as you might expect, a large Victorian house painted red, started its career in 1904, when this part of the city was hardly city at all. Then called the Jefferson Hotel, it opened near the edge

TOP ATTRACTIONS IN THE CENTRAL NEIGHBORHOODS

The Haight-Ashbury	Queen Anne Hotel
Fillmore Auditorium	Pacific Heights

of pastoral Golden Gate Park as a country respite for city dwellers. It continued in a genteel and little-noticed manner until 1967, when the hippies began their descent upon Haight-Ashbury. A group of newly arrived kids from New York took over management of the building and began renting rooms for $15 a night. That rate was per room, however, and at the era's height, newly minted hippies were often cramming in enough people that each only had to put up about $1.50.

When Sami Sunchild bought the place in 1977, Haight-Ashbury had long lost that loving feeling, but she has dedicated herself to creating one place, at least, where the spirit of the '60s lives on. The inn's lobby doubles as The Peace Arts Gallery, with peace-symbol T-shirts, bumper stickers, placemats, and buttons among the collection. If touristing has you all wound up, and you just need a place to chill out, there is always the Red Vic's meditation room, complete with comfy pillows to help you reach that higher plane of consciousness.

If you are going to crash at the Red Vic, choose your room carefully. Each has a very different paint job and decorating principle, some of which might keep you up at night. The green and brown Redwood Room ("dedicated to the preservation of the forests of our earth") is nicely soothing, while the bright orange of the Sunshine Room ("dedicated to caring for the air we breathe") will certainly inspire an early start to your day. For the ultimate retro experience, ask for the Summer of Love Room, where you can lie under a tie-dyed canopy while tuning in to a lava lamp, or the Flower Child Room, adventurously painted with clouds and rainbows. For most rooms, the bathroom is down the hall, but you get a choice of decor for these too. Brush your teeth next to the fish in the Aquarium Bathroom, or look at the mural of a soaring eagle in the Bird's Nest Bathroom. Groovy, man. Call 864–1978 or visit www.redvic.com. Moderate.

The high ground in the Haight-Ashbury is occupied by *Buena Vista Park,* a somewhat wild space that has cleaned up nicely from its post-hippie days as a counterculture campground and drug dealing haven. Its northern edge borders Haight Street near Central Avenue, from where it slopes up quickly to its peak. The climb is worth it, as the "good view" promised in the park's name more than lives up to the billing. From various spots near the top, panoramas peek through openings in the trees, displaying City Hall, the Financial District, Golden Gate Park, the bay, the Pacific Ocean, and Golden Gate Bridge from a spectacular angle.

As you meander through the park, take note of the retaining walls next to the paved walkways. If you look closely at the polished stone, you can sometimes see what appear to be letters carved into the pieces. What you are looking at are gravestones. In 1939, when San Francisco's leaders determined that they were running out of space for development, they mandated the removal of

Ashes to Ashes

San Francisco offers just about everything you could want from a city, with one exception: places to store the dead. This has been this case since 1939, when the city forced the removal of all cemeteries to provide more space for development. This measure opened up more living space in a perpetually crowded city, but it caused a real shake-up in the burial industry. The solution for most was to bury their dead in the nearby town of Colma, where there are said to be more dead people than living. Only two cemeteries remain in San Francisco proper: one next to the city's oldest building, Mission Dolores, and the military cemetery in the Presidio. The one other place to store your loved ones' remains for posterity happens to be one of San Francisco's least-known attractions: the *San Francisco Columbarium* (1 Loraine Court) now operated by the Neptune Society. Even many people who live in its immediate vicinity are unaware of its existence, as its dome is tucked behind houses at the end of a dead-end street (pun absolutely intended). A columbarium, a concept dating back to the Romans, is usually a domed structure with niches to hold the ashes of the dead. San Francisco's version was built in 1898 as an adjunct to the Odd Fellows Cemetery, but when that was dug up, the Columbarium was all that remained.

Over the years, many of San Francisco's prominent citizens have been inurned in the Columbarium, but many of the more than 5,000 niches are still available. Despite the nature of the place, the Columbarium is not dour. The niches are set on three floors around a rotunda. The dome has a window at the top to keep the place well lit, and the walls and columns are painted in light pastel colors. Some of the niches are austere, covered in brass plaques with terse epitaphs. Others are more whimsical, filled with items specific to the deceased, such as sporting goods, portraits, and, in one case, two busts of Elvis Presley. Head groundskeeper Emmitt Watson takes a personal interest in the building and its stories and can answer, or will research the answers to, any visitors' questions. Open Monday through Friday 9:00 A.M. to 4:00 P.M., Saturday and Sunday 10:00 A.M. to 2:00 P.M. Call 752–7892.

Columbarium

all cemeteries in the city. Some graves were moved, but many were left behind to be dug up or covered over. When the park's pathways were being built by the Works Progress Administration, a number of gravestones left behind when the city tore up the nearby Lone Mountain Cemetery were put to use here.

Near Buena Vista Park, Haight Street begins to dip, marking the edge of what is generally known as Haight-Ashbury. The area called the *Lower Haight,* an eclectic area of interesting shops, bars, and restaurants, is conveniently located between the Castro, Hayes Valley, and Western Addition areas.

The contrast between the aforementioned Amoeba Records and *Jack's Record Cellar* (254 Scott Street) could hardly be more pronounced. Whereas Amoeba has CDs of just about every imaginable genre in a well-lit space the size of an aircraft hanger, Jack's just has piles of mostly blues, jazz, and early rock-and-roll LPs crammed into a dusty, dimly lit room. As much as a big record store might have to offer, if you want to find an obscure Motown single or a *Jackie Gleason Presents* record, Jack's is your place. There are rarely more than a few customers in the shop, and those who are there are generally rooting through a rack of 78s looking for the Hank Williams record Jack's just might have. There are records everywhere, many of them recently purchased from private collections and piled up in a corner until the staff gets around to organizing them. Even if you don't own a turntable, it's worth stopping in Jack's just to have a look around. The atmosphere is very subdued, and manager Roy Loney, former member of the band The Flaming Groovies, knows more about Elvis Presley's recordings than anyone around. And for those who don't remember, there is a comfort in the muted sound of record jackets hitting against one another as you flip through them that the rattle of CD cases will never match. At the corner of Page and Scott Streets, one block north of Haight. Open Wednesday through Saturday, noon to 7:00 P.M. Call 431–3047. Muni Buses 6, 7, 16, 66, 71.

One of the Lower Haight's best bars is *Mad Dog in the Fog* (530 Haight Street), a British pub that is a favorite of British expats and those who enjoy drinking with them. The pub's other big draw is British soccer shown via satellite. Because of the vagaries of time zones, most of the matches are on at horrendous hours, like 7:00 A.M. on a Sunday, but the English-style breakfasts they serve up seem to quell the masses. Homesick Brits are happy to get up extra early to wolf down menu offerings like "The Greedy Bastard" (English bacon, sausage, scrambled eggs, baked beans, tomatoes, black pudding, and toast) or the lighter "Thatcher's Thick Head" (just bacon, eggs, and a muffin) while cheering on Arsenal or Aston Villa. Remarkably, a fair number of pints of Guinness get poured at that hour as well. During the more reasonable hours, standard pub fare like shepherd's pie and bangers and mash make a fine accompaniment to the many imported beers. Above all, the British just seem to know how to make a pub fun, and the atmosphere is always festive. There is some form of entertainment on most nights, ranging from DJs to pub quizzes to Beatles cover bands. Call 626–7279 to find out what's on each night. Open Monday through Friday 3:30 P.M. to 2:00 A.M. The standard hours on Saturday and Sunday are 10:00 to 2:00 A.M., but they often open earlier (e.g., 6:00 A.M.) for live soccer. Inexpensive.

To the north of the Lower Haight is an area known as the ***Western Addition,*** a name that makes many people scratch their heads because the neighborhood is located in the middle of the city, in fact with more land to the west of it than to the east. The moniker actually dates back to 1851, when everything west of Van Ness Avenue was unpopulated wilderness. The demographic boom of the Gold Rush had crowded the downtown areas, and planners saw the need to extend the city limits westward. The new area, stretching to what is now Divisadero Street, was named the Western Addition, and city fathers set about developing it. There were squatters on the land, some of whom claimed ownership based on deeds granted by the Mexican government, but in 1855 the city passed the Van Ness Ordinance, which threw out all prior claims to the land.

Streets were graded and housing was built, but the Western Addition remained somewhat sparsely populated for the next half century: in the days before automobiles it seemed too far away from the action downtown. Those feelings changed after the 1906 earthquake and fire, however. The downtown areas had been devastated, but because the main firebreak had been established on Van Ness, the Western Addition survived relatively intact. Many of the displaced were now happy to move to the outskirts, and the district thrived. It also became one of the most ethnically diverse parts of the city, with large numbers of Russians, Chinese, Jews, and Japanese. Most of the ethnic groups kept moving west as the Richmond District was developed, but the Japanese, who were just starting to arrive in large numbers, stayed, and the area became known as Nihonmachi, or "Japantown."

AUTHORS' FAVORITES IN THE CENTRAL NEIGHBORHOODS

Amoeba Music

Buena Vista Park

John Lee Hooker's
Boom Boom Room

Fire Department Museum

The Japanese character of the neighborhood grew until the attack on Pearl Harbor. Military leaders assigned to defend the West Coast were concerned that Japanese-Americans would support their country of origin in the war, and in 1942 President Franklin Roosevelt signed Executive Order 1066, which mandated the relocation of all people of Japanese descent on the West Coast to internment camps in the desert. At the same time that Japanese were being forced to leave their neighborhood and their homes behind, large numbers of blacks were migrating from the southern United States to San Francisco to take jobs building warships. These newcomers weren't welcome in many areas of the city, so they settled on the blocks vacated by the Japanese.

Before long, the Western Addition was home to a thriving black community and one of the United States' great music scenes. In the 1950s the neighborhood had some fifty clubs that became mandatory stops for the great jazz and blues artists of the day. The Fillmore, as the Western Addition is often called, soon gained a reputation as "The Harlem of the West," a major center of African-American culture. This golden age didn't last long because a contemptible "redevelopment" plan forced many black residents from their homes, and the music scene withered away. In recent years, attempts have been made to resuscitate the Fillmore as San Francisco's jazz district, but so far the only sign of a rebirth is *John Lee Hooker's Boom Boom Room* (1601 Fillmore Street).

In 1997, the legendary blues guitarist bought Jack's Bar, the first "black" club in the neighborhood, and renamed it after one of his hit songs, "Boom Boom." It soon became one of San Francisco's favorite nightspots and was written about internationally. Rhythm and blues bands hit the stage every night, and, until his death in 2001, Hooker himself would occasionally show up and play a set. The Boom Boom Room attracts a diverse crowd, including the type of folks who wouldn't have spent much time in the old Fillmore, but it still feels real. The muted lighting, the red vinyl banquettes, and above all, the top-notch acts on stage give the place enough of a sultry, gritty feel to remain cool. In a nice arrangement, the front of the club is taken up by tables and a long bar down one side while the back is devoted to just the stage and the dance floor. This allows for socializing and relaxing in one part and some serious dancing in the other. Open daily 2:00 P.M. to 2:00 A.M. Check newspaper listings, call 673–8000, or visit www.boomboomblues.com to find out what band is playing. Muni Bus 22.

Across Geary Street from the Boom Boom Room is the *Fillmore Auditorium* (1805 Fillmore Street), an important site in the history of San Francisco rock and roll. Originally opened in 1912 as the Majestic Ballroom, during the neighborhood's heyday in the late 1940s and 1950s it hosted concerts by some of the most famous black musicians, including Ray Charles and Billie Holiday. As the neighborhood and musical tastes changed in the mid-'60s, a young concert promoter named Bill Graham began to use the theater for shows by the city's up-and-coming acts, including the Grateful Dead, Santana, Jefferson Airplane, and Big Brother and the Holding Company, as well as international headliners like Pink Floyd and The Who. Damage from the 1989 earthquake closed the Fillmore for four years, but since reopening, it once again holds concerts by big rock acts and headliners. Check listings, call 346–6000, or visit www.thefillmore.com for show information.

For a Western Addition experience that is both musical and spiritual, try **St. John Coltrane African Orthodox Church** (930 Gough Street). Popularly known as the Church of St. John Coltrane, it was founded on the inspiration of the far-out jazzman and puts on one of the wildest Sunday morning shows around. At first blush, John Coltrane seems like an odd choice to base a religion on. The innovative saxophonist known for his wild solos had serious heroin and alcohol problems throughout his career, not exactly making him a candidate for sainthood. Toward the end of his career, however, Coltrane found religion, kicked his addictions, and began to experiment with spirituality in his music. Bishop Franzo King founded the church after seeing Coltrane play in 1965, just two years before the saxophonist died from liver cancer. A multiracial crowd fills the pews for Sunday services, all united by a love of jazz. Some bring instruments and participate in the spiritual jams, while others simply dance in place. Services begin Sunday at noon, but arrive by 11:45 A.M. Call 673–3572, ext. 6, as this location is not considered permanent for the church's ministry, or check www.saintjohncoltrane.com. Muni Bus 16.

At the end of World War II, when Japanese-Americans were released from the internment camps, only a few returned to live in what had been Japantown. For many, the homes they had once lived in were either occupied or no longer there, and they dispersed to other parts of the city and the Bay Area. City leaders felt guilty about the treatment of the Japanese, however, and hoped to recreate a Japantown in the Western Addition. As part of the redevelopment, planners laid out space for a **Japan Center** (www.japantown.ws) to resuscitate the Japanese character of the neighborhood. Several streets were closed off, and a series of indoor malls was built along Geary Street between Fillmore and Gough. The malls were designed to resemble Japanese villages, with authentic Japanese shops set back from "roads" along which people could stroll. The attempt to recreate Japantown, despite a huge white Peace Pagoda, was destined to fail because the Japanese population simply is not the dominant group in the area anymore, but the malls do attract large numbers of

Japanese people from throughout the city. With Japanese record shops, book stores, restaurants, a bakery selling delicious *tai yaki* bean cakes, and organizations like the Ikenobo Ikebana Society of America (devoted to the art of flower arranging) taking up residence, it is a natural draw for Japanese shoppers, especially on weekends. So despite the center's artificial feeling, the malls have enough life and just enough authenticity to merit a visit for a Japanese dinner before a feature film at the complex's multiplex theater.

One of the things that this area of San Francisco is known for is its large collection of well-preserved Victorian architecture, the style in vogue in the late nineteenth century. While good examples can be found in other areas, most notably the Castro and Noe Valley, Pacific Heights and Japantown have the lion's share of the city's roughly 14,000 Victorian homes. In 1906 there were about 50,000 throughout San Francisco, but most of the wooden structures were gobbled up in the fire that followed that year's earthquake. At the turn of the twentieth century, the finest Victorian mansions lined Van Ness Avenue. Sadly, these homes were dynamited by the fire department in order to create a firebreak on that wide boulevard. That action successfully kept the fire away from Pacific Heights and the Western Addition and saved the Victorians you see there today.

thevarietiesofthe victorian

The Victorian movement consisted of three main styles. First, in the 1870s came the Italianate, a relatively simple style with flat fronts and sharp roof cornices. This style tended to feature narrow, arched windows and Corinthian columns. Many Italianate homes followed a similar cookie-cutter design, making them the tract houses of their day. In the 1880s, as mechanization increased, it became easier to make designs with a bit more flourish, and what is known as the stick style began to emerge. Things were still pretty simple, however, until the 1890s, when technology had advanced to the point that builders began pulling out all the stops. In what is known as the Queen Anne style, designers added all sorts of ornamentation, including turrets, gables, and, most ridiculously, fake swallows' nests along the cornices.

A fine example of Victorian architecture at its most exuberant is the **Queen Anne Hotel** (1590 Sutter Street) on the edge of Japantown. Built in 1890 by James Fair, the silver baron for whom Nob Hill's Fairmont Hotel is named, the mansion was for a time the home of a "school for young ladies" and later a women's boardinghouse before its current incarnation as a hotel. With its four peaked roofs and central turret, the building's pink-hued exterior embodies the Queen Anne spirit, but you need to go inside for the full effect. The salon is appointed with carved wood furniture and heavy velvet drapes that were cut long so as to bunch up on the floor, blocking drafts. The rooms themselves are not enormous, but each is equipped with period furniture, and many have fireplaces and bay windows with views. Call 441–2828 or visit www.queenanne.com for more information. Expensive.

Somewhere around Sutter Street, as the streets begin to slope upward, Japantown and the Western Addition begin to give way to *Pacific Heights,* one of the fanciest parts of the city. This is truly where the other half lives, or perhaps the other one-half of 1 percent. The streets are full of mansions, some turned into museums and others still single-family homes. Pacific Heights peaks at Broadway, where the streets drop as abruptly as the law allows. Driving across Broadway on a street like Divisadero gives you that feeling of being in the front car of a roller coaster, hanging over the edge for an instant before you start going down. The streets are so steep at this point, in fact, that as you start down, for a moment you can't even see the road in front of you. If you are brave enough to give it a try, just take it on faith that your tires will maintain contact with pavement while you enjoy the breathtaking sight of the glittering bay and all that surrounds it. This is also a good place to walk and snap pictures. It's a steep route down to Cow Hollow and the Marina, so most of the sidewalks have stairs cut into them to prevent pedestrians from rolling down several blocks.

Perhaps the most interesting musical experience to be found in San Francisco is neither in the Symphony Hall nor in a hip South of Market club. It might instead be found in an obscure theater behind the storefront of an old bakery on the edge of Pacific Heights. On Friday evening at *Audium* (1616 Bush Street), audiences sit in seats laid out in concentric circles and wait for the lights to go down. When the room has reached near complete darkness (with only a few faint arrows on the floor to point out the exit) the 169 speakers arrayed throughout the room begin to emit sound. Some of it resembles what we think of as music, most of it synthesized, but the rest is ambient sound, such as waves crashing on a beach or the low murmur of conversation. The sounds are all prerecorded, but maestro Stan Shaff moves them from speaker to speaker live, changing the experience as the various sounds move about the room. The idea of the darkness is to free the listener from the tyranny of sight, so he or she can give full attention to listening. An added effect is that your mind will tend to conjure up images out of the music much more interesting than anything you've seen at the Pink Floyd laser light show. Performances start at 8:30 P.M. every Friday and Saturday, but arrive at 8:00 while the lights are still on. Admission for those over eleven years old is $12. Call 771–1616 or visit www.audium.org for more information and reservations.

As we saw with Buena Vista Park, in devising the layout of San Francisco's streets, city planners had the brilliant foresight to reserve some of the best-placed plots as parkland. Nowhere is this better exemplified than in **Alta Plaza Park** (between Jackson, Clay, Scott, and Steiner Streets), a beloved hump of green space in the middle of Pacific Heights. To be sure, the finer Pacific Heights mansions occupy some prime real estate, but take a gander at the view from the top of this park, and you can just bet that developers salivated at this spot.

high-classthrift

As Fillmore Street rises in elevation, from the traditionally working-class Western Addition to wealthy Pacific Heights, its shops also become ritzier. Interestingly enough, however, this stretch of Fillmore is also notable for its secondhand and thrift shops, where some of the city's wealthiest families donate last season's fashions. While some shops are for profit, a few that donate their proceeds to charity often have the fanciest stuff. *Repeat Performance* (2436 Fillmore Street) benefits the San Francisco Symphony and usually has like-new ball gowns. Open Monday through Saturday 10:00 A.M. to 5:30 P.M. Call 563–3123. If they don't have what you're looking for, across the street is the Junior League's **Next-to-New-Shop** (2226 Fillmore Street), open Monday through Saturday 10:00 A.M. to 5:30 P.M., Sunday noon to 4:00 P.M., benefiting the women's philanthropic organization. Call 567–1627.

One of the best places for a meal in Pacific Heights is **Jackson Fillmore** (2506 Fillmore Street). The Italian trattoria is both small and popular, and it takes reservations only for parties of three or more, so plan on a delay. On a weekend evening, you would sometimes think it was the only restaurant in the neighborhood. Diners cram into the few tables and fill the bar seats, overlooking the chefs preparing their antipasti. Then there are those looking for a table, standing in every open space while dodging the staff. The waiting seems to be half the fun for some, as they order a bottle of wine and drink the contents while standing on the sidewalk out front. The real reason for the crowds, though, is the quality of the food. While you are contemplating the menu, you are given a plate of crostini, toasted bread under a tomato, garlic, and olive oil mixture. These are on the house, and if you're not in love with the place already, wait for the main dishes. The recipes are mostly simple but interesting, with a host of tasty pasta dishes and succulent fish. A recommended choice is the delightfully sweet pumpkin ravioli. Open Sunday through Thursday 5:30 to 9:30 P.M., Friday and Saturday until 10:30 P.M. Call 346–5288. Moderate.

In San Francisco's early days, devastating fires were regular events, coming as surely as the changing of the seasons. When gold was discovered and people from all over the world started arriving in 1849, there was little time or inclination to build proper housing for everyone. People were living in ramshackle wooden houses, often constructed from the hulls of broken-down ships and covered with canvas to keep out the elements. A city of such dwellings was a natural habitat for fires, and between January 1849 and July 1851, six major fires swept through the city, at great cost in lives and property. The catastrophic conflagration that remained a constant threat throughout the next half century finally came to pass in 1906. Given its huge importance in the city's history, it is surprising that the *Fire Department Museum* (655 Presidio Avenue between Bush and Pine Streets) is so obscurely located that few native San Franciscans even know it is there.

On the left as you enter the museum is a bell about 5 feet in diameter that once hung in Chinatown's Portsmouth Square. When the department was all volunteer, the bell would be rung when a fire broke out to summon any able-bodied men to help extinguish it. In 1906, however, the earthquake dropped it to the ground. Much worse news for the firefighting effort on that day, the fire department's chief engineer had been mortally injured during the tremor. Dennis T. Sullivan was asleep in the official chief's quarters in a firehouse on Bush Street on the morning of April 18 when the earth shook. The dome of the California Hotel next door crashed through the building, causing him to fall through the floor of the room and into the cellar. Firefighters and volunteers began to dig through the rubble when, according to one witness, the chief walked out from behind the pile. He had suffered a fractured skull, several broken ribs, and a punctured lung and was badly scalded by water from a radiator he had landed near. He died after four days in the hospital.

Some of the museum's claims are admittedly a bit dubious, such as the story of a firefighter named Tom Sawyer. As the story goes, this Tom Sawyer made the acquaintance of a young newspaper reporter who wrote under the name Mark Twain, and the rest was history. No Twain scholar has been able to confirm the accuracy of this tale, but it's a yarn the author might have appreciated just the same. Open Thursday through Sunday 1:00 to 4:00 P.M. Admission is free. Call 563–4630 during museum hours or 558–3546 for voice mail or visit www.sffiremuseum.org. Muni Buses 2, 4, 43.

Places to Stay in the Central Neighborhoods

The Archbishop's Mansion Inn
1000 Fulton Street
563–7872
www.jdvhospitality.com/hotels/hotel/2
It takes a lot to live up to such a name, but the Archbishop's Mansion does that and then some. For forty-one years, from 1904 to 1945, this was the home of three consecutive archbishops of San Francisco, and you can't help but envy the guys a little bit. From the lobby to the rooms, this is about as elegant as it gets, and the location in the boutique Alamo Square District puts it close to the Civic Center and Pacific Heights. Expensive.

Hotel Drisco
2901 Pacific Avenue
346–2880
www.hoteldrisco.com
For those with a taste for extremely high-end accommodations, a stay in this former Pacific Heights men's club should fit the bill. The views alone make the Drisco worth an endorsement, although it is somewhat isolated in a residential neighborhood. Expensive.

The Metro Hotel
319 Divisadero Street
861–5364
www.metrohotelsf.com
This simple but comfortable hotel is popular with the European backpacking crowd. Perfect for travelers who want to sleep away from the touristy areas, the Metro is also centrally located within walking distance of the Haight and the Castro. The rooms are pleasant, if unmemorable. The favorite feature is the garden patio in back, where you can order food from the adjoining restaurant and shoot the breeze with fellow guests. Inexpensive.

Radisson Miyako Hotel
1625 Post Street
922–3200
www.miyakohotel.com
This is a chain hotel like no other, anchoring one end of the Japan Center. Ask for a room with a Japanese-style soaking tub, stroll the hotel's Japanese garden with colorful koi in a pond, and feel the virtual warmth in front of the Lord of Balls Lounge holographic fireplace. Moderate.

Stanyan Park Hotel
750 Stanyan Street
751–1000
www.stanyanpark.com
The oldest hotel along the rim of Golden Gate Park, the Stanyan Park's simple but elegant Victorian rooms, including a Cupola Room, provide a relaxing respite from the city. However, Haight Street is just around the corner, so you are far from isolated. Moderate.

Places to Eat in the Central Neighborhoods

Cha! Cha! Cha!
1801 Haight Street
386–7670
Spicy dishes like Caribbean jerk chicken and Cajun shrimp have made this one of the Haight-Ashbury's favorite restaurants. It can be very crowded on weekends, and the restaurant does not take reservations, so be prepared to spend some time at the bar. Open Sunday through Thursday 11:30 A.M. to 4:00 P.M.. 5:00 P.M. to 11:00 P.M., Friday and Saturday 5:00 to 11:30 P.M. Moderate.

Eliza's
2877 California Street
621–4819
Bustling Hunan-Mandarin Chinese fusion—attitude and cuisine—with lines out the front door and a luminous use of glass to gussy up wall decor rev up down-to-earth destination dining on the edge of Pacific Heights. Ostrich with Chinese garlic or mango is just one of the combos. Open Monday through Friday 11:00 A.M. to 3:00 P.M. and 5:00 P.M. to 9:45 P.M., Saturday and Sunday 4:30 to 9:45 P.M. Moderate.

Eos
901 Cole Street
566–3063
www.eossf.com
One of San Francisco's most highly praised restaurants, Eos is located in the quiet neighborhood of Cole Valley, close to the Haight-Ashbury. The menu is mostly Asian fusion, but expect a little bit of everything. Eos is very popular, so call for a reservation. Open Sunday through Thursday 5:30 to 10:00 P.M., Friday and Saturday until 11:00 P.M. Expensive.

Isobune
1737 Post Street
563–1030
The fish at this sushi restaurant is not only raw, it's moving. Diners sit around a little river, on which float little boats carrying different varieties of sushi. When you see something you like, reach in and grab it as it goes by. If your favorite isn't showing up, or if some guy upstream keeps snagging it, just ask the chefs working in the center and they'll make you a special plate. Eat as much or as little as you like. Servers will tally your bill on the basis of the number of different colored plates you amass. Located in the Japan Center's Kinetsu Mall. Open daily 11:30 A.M. to 10:00 P.M. Moderate.

Magnolia Pub & Brewery
1398 Haight Street
864–7468
www.magnoliapub.com
The chef uses local artisan bread, local oysters, and organic beef to marry with the ten or so brews served on tap, including the rave-reviewed Stout of Circumstance. A mouthwatering juicy burger on focaccia is just the fortification needed before strolling where the Summer of Love began. Open Monday through Thursday noon to midnight, Friday noon to 1:00 A.M., Saturday 10:00 to 1:00 A.M., Sunday 10:00 A.M. to 11:30 P.M. Moderate.

The Castro and the Mission

The Castro and Mission Districts, two of San Francisco's most interesting and distinct, sit side by side south of Upper Market Street. A good place to get a bird's-eye view of the neighborhood is **Corona Heights,** a little-visited rocky outcropping just to the north. To get there, take 14th Street up the hill from Divisadero, and follow the signs.

Perched on Corona Heights, the ***Randall Museum*** (199 Museum Way) is a little-known haven for animals unable to survive in the wild and one of the best places in the city to bring the kids. While the Academy of Sciences in Golden Gate Park (in temporary quarters in SOMA until 2008) is usually jammed with enough youngsters to make you want to scream, the Randall, holding only about one hundred animals, is generally quieter. You might first notice that the museum's collection of creatures is somewhat unorthodox, including, as it does, a tank of "domestic rats." Then you look up at the red-tailed hawk, a predator indigenous to the Bay Area, and notice that there is no cage separating you and him. The same goes for the great horned owl, who also eyes you calmly from his perch as you walk by. Don't fear a Hitchcockian avian assault. These guys have permanent wing injuries that keep them from

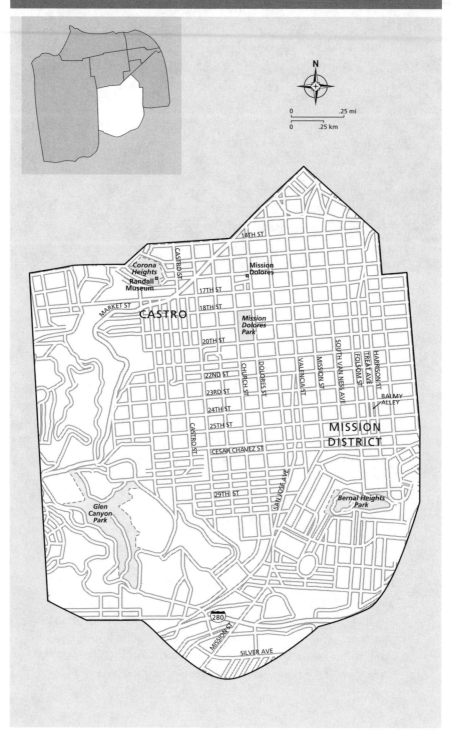

N

0   .25 mi

0   .25 km

14TH ST

Corona Heights

Randall Museum

Mission Dolores

CASTRO ST

MARKET ST

17TH ST

18TH ST

CASTRO

20TH ST

Mission Dolores Park

22ND ST

23RD ST

24TH ST

25TH ST

CHURCH ST

DOLORES ST

VALENCIA ST

MISSION ST

SOUTH VAN NESS AVE

FOLSOM ST

TREAT AVE

HARRISON ST

BALMY ALLEY

CASTRO ST

CESAR CHAVEZ ST

MISSION DISTRICT

SAN JOSE AVE

29TH ST

Glen Canyon Park

Bernal Heights Park

280

MISSION ST

SILVER AVE

too much strenuous activity, so they spend most of their time sitting on their perches trying to look tough.

Even though the animals aren't particularly animated, especially the eight large stone animal sculptures by the late Benny Bufano, the lack of barriers makes for an experience more intimate than one at the zoo. Thankfully, the museum's insect collections are kept behind glass, and kids will love peering in at the stinkbugs, velvet ants, and Costa Rican wood roaches. There is also an impressive working beehive, with a tube that lets the bees pour into the outside world to do their pollinating business. In the museum's basement is the headquarters of the Golden Gate Model Railroad Club. On Saturday from 11:00 A.M. to 4:00 P.M., they turn the trains on for public viewing. Open Tuesday through Saturday 10:00 A.M. to 5:00 P.M. Admission is free but donations are encouraged. Call 554–9600 or visit www.randallmuseum.org.

Once a nondescript, working-class Irish neighborhood known as Eureka Valley, the area around Castro Street began to change in the 1970s when gays from around the city began buying and restoring the beautiful Victorian homes that had fallen into disrepair a decade earlier. San Francisco has had a gay culture for as long it has had any culture, seeing as how some 95 percent of the forty-niners were men. For most of that time, the gay lifestyle had to be kept underground, but unofficial gay bars thrived in many parts of the city. Several neighborhoods, most notably Polk Street and Haight-Ashbury, were home to large gay populations, but migration to the Castro, as Eureka Valley soon came to be known, was something new. Rather than just finding peace in other open-minded communities, gays developed their own community unlike anywhere else in the world. Today's **Castro District** has the feel of an ethnic neighborhood, where the ethnicity happens to be gay. The neighborhood's buildings are lovingly maintained, the streets are safe, and, more so than in other areas of the city, people seem to know each other. Because of this, the Castro has even begun to attract heterosexual families who value the tightly knit community.

At the corner of Market and Castro Streets, above the underground Muni Metro station, is **Harvey Milk Plaza.** Here a giant 20-by-30-foot rainbow flag,

TOP ATTRACTIONS IN THE CASTRO AND THE MISSION

Harvey Milk Plaza

Castro Theatre

Mission San Francisco de Asis (Mission Dolores)

Dolores Park

a gay emblem, flapping overhead on a 70-foot flagpole, announces the neighborhood's character with pride. Harvey Milk was one of the Castro's most important figures, a political leader who met a tragic end. A local community activist campaigning out of his Castro Street camera shop, Milk won election to the board of supervisors (San Francisco's equivalent of a city council) in 1977 and gained fame as the first openly gay elected official in the country. He became known in the neighborhood as "The Mayor of Castro Street" and seemed to personify the San Francisco gay community's newfound self-confidence. Along with sympathetic Mayor George Moscone, Milk helped pass the city's first law guaranteeing civil rights to gays.

The tragedy struck on November 27, 1978. Dan White, a conservative supervisor upset at losing his seat on the board, stormed into City Hall, first shooting Moscone in the mayor's office, then walking across the rotunda to assassinate Milk in his office. The Castro, and the city as a whole, went into mourning, and awaited what seemed like a sure murder conviction and lifetime prison sentence for White. The assassin's lawyers, however, argued that White's brain was addled at the time of the shootings because he had eaten too much junk food. Shockingly, the jury bought the so-called "Twinkie Defense." On May 21, 1979, they returned a lesser verdict of manslaughter, which would allow White to be released in as little as six years.

Thousands of outraged gay people marched from the Castro to the Civic Center in a protest that quickly turned violent. Protesters smashed City Hall's windows and set fire to about a dozen police cars in what became known as the "White Night Riot." Just after midnight, the police decided to ride to the

Following in the Footsteps of Harvey

Harvey Milk is in many ways a founding father of the Castro, the Abraham Lincoln of gay San Francisco. His activism, election to city government, and tragic death defined an era for the Castro and led to greater political involvement among gay people. As a result, Milk's name is all over the neighborhood. Besides the plaza that bears his name and Harvey's bar and restaurant, those who want to make a Milk pilgrimage can visit the former site of the camera shop owned by Milk and his partner. Milk ran his campaign for supervisor from *Castro Camera* (575 Castro Street), inviting residents to come in, sit on his couch, and tell him their concerns about life in the city. The camera store is long gone, having been forced out by rising rents in the late 1970s, but a sidewalk plaque marks the spot, and a portrait of Milk with the quote "You gotta give 'em hope" can be seen through the second-floor window. A block west is the *Harvey Milk Civil Rights Academy* (4235 19th Street), an alternative public elementary school that teaches nonviolence and tolerance.

AUTHORS' FAVORITES IN THE CASTRO AND THE MISSION

Randall Museum	Balmy Alley
Castro Theatre	Bernal Heights Park
Dolores Park	

Castro to exact some revenge. Cops in riot gear confronted the crowd at Castro and 18th Streets—known locally as "The Gayest Four Corners on Earth"—and charged into a popular bar called the Elephant Walk. The officers spent ten minutes swinging their nightsticks wildly, trashing the place and seriously injuring several employees and patrons. In a strange coincidence, this horrible event, the worst episode of violence in the short history of the Castro, took place in the early hours of the day on which Harvey Milk would have turned forty-nine. After cleaning up the mess that the cops left behind, Castro residents gathered at the intersection of Castro and 18th Streets to sing "Happy Birthday." The Elephant Walk is now a restaurant and bar named *Harvey's* (431–4278). Its window tables, usually difficult to score, provide the best place possible to watch the wonder that is the Castro.

Truth be told, while Castro Street is a marvel, it's also somewhat touristy, and its numerous tacky shops selling sex toys and T-shirts bearing lewd sayings designed to shock the folks back home can wear thin quickly. There are, however, several unique establishments on the street not the least of which is *Cliff's Variety* (479 Castro Street), one of the nicest hardware stores around. Originally a five-and-dime store in the old Irish Eureka Valley, the family that owned Cliff's saw the way the neighborhood was changing in the 1970s and adjusted accordingly. Not only was it one of the first straight-owned businesses to hire gays, it soon began to cater to their needs and tastes. One of the things that had first attracted gays to the Castro were the rows and rows of Victorian houses that lined the district's blocks. Many of these had been allowed to deteriorate by previous owners and could be acquired cheaply. The new owners took to renovating the old ladies with aplomb, adding the ornate trimmings and adventurous paint jobs that are the neighborhood rule today. The owners of Cliff's realized that these eager renovators would need a place to buy supplies, and they created the upscale hardware store you see today. The aisles are as pleasantly lit as a fine clothing boutique and filled with all the paints and fixtures and accessories needed to appoint your home.

Open Monday through Saturday 9:30 A.M. to 8:00 P.M.; Sunday 11:00 A.M. to 5:00 P.M. Call 431–5365.

Just up the street is the prime attraction on Castro: the *Castro Theatre* (429 Castro Street). The last of the city's great art deco movie palaces, it consistently draws movie lovers from around the city and the region. Architect Timothy Pflueger, who designed other theaters in the Bay Area, fashioned the outside to look like a Moorish castle, and the handmade tiles of the stand-alone ticket office are the originals. The Castro has undergone several refurbishments in the last few decades, but the interior hasn't changed much, from the sculpted plaster ceiling to the classical murals along the walls. One change that regulars didn't object to was the recent replacement of the previously torturous seats. Adding to the fun of a movie at the Castro is the moving organ below the screen. Just before show time, a mechanism lifts the Wurlitzer up in front of the audience, and the house organist treats them to a prescreening recital of show tunes and, on most nights, "San Francisco."

Catching a film at the Castro is always an event and a huge contrast to the experience at the antiseptic metroplexes that have replaced its contemporaries. Most of the screenings at the Castro are one-off showings of small independent films or rereleases of classics. San Francisco is a city of cineastes, and many of them will usually be lined up well before show time. Pick up a calendar of events in front of the theater or in cafes and bars around the city, call 621–6120 or visit www.thecastrotheatre.com to find out what's showing. In general, it's best to arrive well in advance of show time, especially during one of the many film festivals held at the theater. Retrospectives are gala events, with the featured film's star or director on hand to talk about the filmmaking process and answer questions.

A Castro watering hole of historical significance is *Twin Peaks* (401 Castro Street), the first openly gay bar in the city. When it opened in 1973, gay bars usually had their windows boarded up to prevent pedestrians and police from looking inside and identifying the patrons. Twin Peaks changed all that, however, leaving its panoramic windows uncovered so that the entire bar was visible from the sidewalk. This shocking frankness, at the busy intersection of Castro, 17th, and Market Streets, signaled an emerging confidence in the San Francisco gay community. It is a sign of how far the community has come that such openness is no longer unique. Twin Peaks is usually populated by well-dressed Financial District types of a certain age, often fresh off the Muni after work. Open daily noon to 2:00 A.M. Call 864–9470.

Another great only-in-the-Castro shop is *Medium Rare Records* (2310 Market Street). Owners Sean Connors and Arnold Conrad have focused on certain, mostly campy, genres they are passionate about, and it shows. Their selection of lounge, pop, and jazz vocals and movie and show soundtracks is second to none, and it reflects their personal touch. Many of the items are rare recordings that Sean and Arnold get from distributors whose names they will not reveal. Ask to listen to any CD, and you can take it into the private listening booth in back.

The walls of the store are covered with the images of pop icons, from Sinatra to Cher, but the real patron saint of the shop is jazz singer Peggy Lee. Her CD library takes up the corner nearest the register, and her picture graces the store's publicity cards. Sean and Arnold have a particular affinity for her music, and they seem to have just about everything she ever recorded, no matter how rare. If you have a half hour or so on your hands, ask them about Peggy; they'll be glad to play you a few tunes and tell you her life story. Open Sunday through Thursday 11:00 A.M. to 9:00 P.M., Friday and Saturday noon to 8:00 P.M. Call 255-7273.

There are myriad bars and clubs in the neighborhood, but the best spot in the Castro to see and be seen is *Cafe Flore* (2298 Market Street). One step inside and you'll realize that this isn't the sort of place where people in their sweats roll in half asleep for their Sunday morning coffee. Even if the night before was Halloween or the Gay Pride Parade (the Castro's high holidays, the latter also referenced by its full name, the San Francisco Lesbian, Gay, Bisexual, Transgender Pride Parade), no one comes to Cafe Flore without carefully choosing his apparel and properly adjusting his hair. The scene notwithstanding, Cafe Flore is a very comfortable spot in which to hang out any time of day. Besides the coffee, the cubicle of a kitchen churns out tasty meals all day long, from breakfast frittatas to sandwiches of chicken liver pâté. Since beer and wine are also served, Cafe Flore is the sort of place you don't feel compelled to leave right away, as evidenced by the customers who seem to spend all day there, flipping through a book of philosophy or doodling in a sketchbook. The cafe's interior is pleasant, with sturdy wooden tables under a peaked corrugated tin roof and plenty of hanging plants, but if the weather is nice, the outside tables are at a premium. Open daily 7:00 A.M. to 11:00 P.M., Friday and Saturday until midnight. Call 621-8579. Inexpensive.

To enter a proper speakeasy, you really should have to walk through a dark corridor, or at least descend a steep staircase the way you do to enter *Cafe du Nord* (2170 Market Street). The nature of the place is no longer subrosa, of course, but there is something about the descent that still imparts the thrill of doing something vaguely illicit. Parts of the interior evoke its earlier incarnation, particularly the dim lighting and the deep red wainscoting on the walls. Cafe du Nord really consists of two parts: the lounge, with a well-stocked bar and comfortable couches, and the showroom, where an eclectic list of performers hits the stage on most nights. Check the listings before you go. One night might feature a salsa band, the next night country-western, and the night after that a gay comedy/cooking show (seriously!). On Friday night the stage may be occupied by Lavay Smith and Her Red Hot Skillet Lickers, a swing and blues band that always packs the room. The cafe's menu includes burgers, spicy chicken, kabobs, ahi (tuna), and Thai-style calimari. Open Sunday through Tuesday 6:00 P.M. to 2:00 A.M., Wednesday through Saturday 4:00 P.M. to 2:00 A.M. Call 861–5016 or visit www.cafedunord.com. Inexpensive.

There doesn't seem to be any official dividing line between the Castro and the *Mission District,* but for our purposes the change happens somewhere between Church and Dolores Streets. Whether this border indicates a cultural change anymore is up for debate, but because Dolores Street is home to the place that gives the Mission District its name, it is the most logical spot to mark the change. The place in question is *Mission San Francisco de Asis* (Dolores at 3371 16th Street), widely known as Mission Dolores. The adobe structure is San Francisco's oldest building, erected by Spanish missionaries whose religious fervor was enough to drive them to this windswept wasteland. In the 1770s, the Spanish monarchs, concerned about Russian traders moving down from Alaska, mandated the establishment of twenty-one missions along the California coast to the north of Spanish-controlled Mexico. A party was dispatched to find a suitable locale on the San Francisco peninsula, and the first mass was held near the current spot on June 29, 1776, five days before the folks back east signed the Declaration of Independence.

The very first mission was somewhat hastily assembled at the confluence of two streams that then flowed through the undeveloped area. So unsuitable was it to the often rough climes of San Francisco that the stiff wet winds blew

Mission San Francisco de Asis

it down. Construction was soon commenced on a sturdier mission building at the present site. The religious purpose of the mission was to convert the area's native Ohlone Indians and, from the start, the missionaries put the natives to work. They stomped out the clay for the 36,000 adobe bricks, each 4 feet thick, before laying them to dry in the sun. While a good deal of work has been done on the mission building over the years, it is still mostly intact and much the way it was at the beginning. The chapel's main altar was brought from Mexico in 1796; the two side altars followed in 1810. Some burial plots inside the chapel also add an interesting element, as a few of the stone markers were incorporated into the tile floor.

The rest of the burial plots are in the cemetery around the back of the mission, one of two burial grounds left in San Francisco. Most of the original grave markers from the Spanish days are gone; the oldest one remaining dates from the 1800s. Headstones can be found for Luis Antonio Arguello, the first Mexican governor of Alta California; Don Francisco de Haro, the first Mexican alcalde (mayor) of San Francisco; and James Casey, Charles Cora, and James Sullivan, who were hanged by the Vigilance Committee that ran the streets in 1856. Behind the mission's cemetery is an innocuous-looking parking lot, but it is believed that under the concrete are the unmarked graves of some 5,000 Ohlones, most of whom died of European diseases against which they had no defense.

Next to the squat mission is the towering **Mission Basilica,** completed in 1918 after the 1906 earthquake destroyed the first parish church. It wasn't officially a basilica (an honorary church of the Pope) until the Vatican named it as such in 1952. A papal coat of arms to the left of the altar and a red-and-gold umbrella that sits half opened to the right are the official symbols of a basilica. The Pope didn't actually pay a visit until 1987, an event that is well documented photographically in the corridors. The basilica is really quite striking, both inside and out. The outside keeps with the Spanish Revival style popular in the early twentieth century, its brown and green tiled domes distinguishing it from the other buildings around it. Inside, take note of the lovely stained-glass window depicting St. Francis of Assisi, for whom the mission and the city were named, and the sky-blue hue of the dome's interior, which reflects sunlight gently from the skylight at the peak. Open daily 9:00 A.M. to 4:00 P.M., to 4:30 P.M. spring and summer. Suggested donation for children is $2.00, for adults $3.00. Call 621–8203 or visit www.californiamissions.com/cahistory/dolores.html.

Two blocks south of the mission on Dolores Street is **Dolores Park.** The only significant green space in the area, it's always full on sunny days. The park, only one block square, slopes up rapidly to its southwest corner, giving that spot a fantastic view of downtown San Francisco. The J-Church Muni Metro streetcar lets passengers off at this point, in case you're not in a hill-climbing mood. Dolores Park is also home to a flock of wild parrots, which roost in its trees between forays around the city. The parrots, immortalized in Armistead Maupin's book *Tales of the City,* are believed to have escaped from homes after being imported from South America as pets.

This spot is not only picturesque, it is also important to the history of the neighborhood. After the 1906 earthquake, fire engulfed almost everything you can see from here and threatened to climb the hill and destroy this neighbor-hood too. A firebreak was created on Dolores Street, whereby every building on the east side of that wide thoroughfare was summarily dynamited. It helped, but a desperate water shortage made the firefighters' jobs nearly impossible. To defend the area west of Dolores, they relied on a single fire hydrant at the corner of Church and 20th Streets, which pumped enough to stanch the fire's flow. Each April 18, the anniversary of the quake, volunteers gather at the hydrant, giving it a fresh coat of gold paint in honor of its efforts.

On Valencia Street near Market you will find the wooden-front former **Levi Strauss Factory** (250 Valencia Street), rebuilt after the 1906 earthquake in the city where the famous jeans were born. It is well known among San Franciscans that the people who made the most money during the Gold Rush were not the prospectors themselves but the people who sold the ore-seekers the things they needed to keep going. (Many in today's Mission District would probably see a parallel to the Internet gold rush of the nineties that left workers with worthless stock options but landlords and trendy restaurant owners laughing all the way to the bank.) The prime example of this phenomenon was Levi Strauss, an orphaned German immigrant who saw and exploited a need, thereby creating one of the most enduring American brands. As we went to press, no one had announced what Levi's plans to do with the old building. Whether Levi's turns its former flagship factory into a museum or not, Levi's lives on in San Francisco in a techno-chrome store on Union Square.

Working in the American west as a traveling cloth salesman, Strauss made his way to California when gold was discovered. He had brought with him a supply of canvas, intending to sell it for the production of covered wagons. Upon arriving in the gold country, he saw how hard prospecting was on miners' trousers, so he began to cut and sew his canvas into pants. These quickly became popular among the miners for their durability, and Strauss set up a proper company in San Francisco. The basic design has stayed pretty much the same from those first days, with a few exceptions. For one, the fledgling company decided to switch from canvas to a fabric called *serge de Nîmes,* eventually known as "denim." It is also said the original design featured a metal rivet, like the ones still found on the pockets, that secured the jeans' crotch, but it was removed because it tended to heat up when the wearer sat next to a fire, causing intense discomfort.

Discomfort is the last thing on anyone's mind at **Foreign Cinema** (2534 Mission Street), where art films are projected on exterior walls in the evening. For many, a showing of Antonioni's 1966 classic *Blow Up* or 2003's *The Animatrix,* a series of short Japanese animated features inspired by the worldwide hit film *The Matrix,* is only an excuse to arrive early at the busy bar and sample

Bear vs. Bull

In the rough-and-tumble days of the Gold Rush, the land across the street from the Mission Dolores was used for decidedly unreligious purposes. In the Spanish tradition, a bullring was set up, but the action there wasn't limited to the usual red-cape-and-olé affairs. The operators, melding the frontier spirit with old-world tradition, often staged bouts between bulls and bears. A bear would be chained to a post in the center of the ring, and a bull, made angry by darts shot into its side, would attack it. No records are left to determine which creature usually got the better of these contests, but they were certainly violent. Even lawless San Francisco was appalled, and in 1854 protesters had the ring shut down.

cuisine that started out French and has branched broadly into Mediterranean-style dishes inspired by France, Spain, and Italy. The mixed grill entree is an example: Moroccan spiced quail, duck breast, liver crostini, treviso, cracklings, almonds, figs, and honey. Thirteen varieties of oysters support the trendy hotspot's claim that the food is sexy, simple, enduring, and restorative. North-ern halibut is served in a fig leaf. Even the drink menu enjoys an arch wink: a French Kiss, as the brunch menu says, "for the early riser," combines chilled Grey Goose vodka, a "kiss" of Lillet, and a splash of Billecart-Salmon Brut Reserve Champagne. Open Tuesday through Thursday 5:30 to 10:00 P.M., Fri-day to 11:00 P.M., Saturday 11:30 A.M. to 11:00 P.M., Sunday 11:00 A.M. to 9:00 P.M. Call 648-7600 or visit www.foreigncinema.com.

Even with the much bemoaned gentrification of recent years, the Mission District remains predominantly Latino, as it has been for the last half century. The neighborhood does have a history of changing ethnicities, however. In the first half of the twentieth century, after the 1906 quake left much of North Beach in rubble, many of that neighborhood's Italians took up residence in the Mis-sion. Heavy immigration from Mexico and Central and South America began in the 1950s, and the Italian presence began to dwindle to the point where today it is almost unnoticeable. One place left over from those days is *Lucca Ravioli Company* (1100 Valencia Street at 22nd Street), seemingly unchanged since they began making pasta here in 1917. Hunks of cheese still hang by rope from the ceiling, large men in white aprons and hats still banter with customers as they bang out the prices on an ancient manual register, and shoppers still jostle for position in the narrow aisles. Lucca's ravioli are legendary, especially the meat, cheese, and spinach variety made for the Thanksgiving season. Through the deli's Valencia Street window, watch the ravioli and pasta makers lovingly handling the dough in a surprisingly tiny space. While waiting to be served, customers look up at the ceiling mural of Italy, while the owner, Mike, who often waits on customers himself, proudly tells the story of the mural and his ancestors' migration from the Lucca region of Northern Italy. Don't miss out on the delicious deli smells while standing in the tiny aisles. Regardless of how the neighborhood changes, people will make special trips just to come here. Open Monday through Saturday 9:00 A.M. to 6:00 P.M. Call 647–5581.

San Francisco offers the food lover many choices. In addition to providing fine cuisine from every country on earth, it is the home of that culinary phenomenon known as "California cuisine." Despite all the highbrow choices, the one food item many San Franciscans miss the most when they are away is the Mission-style burrito. For those who have not yet had the pleasure, the burrito is a heavenly mélange of rice, beans, cheese, sour cream, avocado, tomato salsa, and some type of meat folded into a hot flour tortilla. Originally invented for laborers in Mexico as a way to consolidate a complete meal into one easy-to-carry item, the burrito was raised to an art form in the taquerias of the Mission District.

While all San Franciscans agree that the best burrito is to be found in the Mission, they rarely agree on which of the several shops makes the best. That debate may never end, but the choice here is **El Farolito** (2779 Mission Street). The food comes in plastic baskets, the tables are usually sticky, and the rest room is always a risky proposition, but the food more than makes up for it. The burritos are made with fresh avocado slices, unlike the guacamole other places use, and meat choices range from the expected—steak, grilled chicken, marinated pork—to the frightening: tongue and beef brains. The crowd that is usually lined up outside isn't there just for the burritos, however. Another unbeatable item is the quesadilla suiza, thinly sliced grilled steak with melted cheese between two tortillas. El Farolito is open after bars close at 2:00 A.M. Hours are Sunday through Thursday 10:00 to 1:00 A.M., Friday and Saturday until 2:45 A.M. Call 824–7877. Inexpensive.

From El Farolito, turn left and stroll down **24th Street,** the historic **Corazon de la Mission,** "the heart of the mission." In contrast to grungy Mission Street, 24th is a clean, tree-lined stretch full of bakeries, restaurants, shops, and galleries. Another of the Mission District's hallmarks is the vast number of murals that cover many of its walls. Throughout the sprawling district, neighborhood artists have decorated buildings in vibrant colors, making some of the streets resemble outdoor art galleries. While you are on the main drag, poke your head into **Precita Eyes Mural Arts Center** (2981 24th Street). This is the home of the organization that oversees the district's public arts projects, which also offers great walking tours of the works, complete with explanations of the cultural reference points in the art. The center is open Monday through Friday

10:00 A.M. to 5:00 P.M., Saturday 10:00 A.M. to 4:00 P.M., Sunday noon to 4:00 P.M. Call 285–2287 or visit www.precitaeyes.org for tour schedules.

There are murals everywhere, on schools and churches and stores, but the highest concentration is in *Balmy Alley,* which runs from 24th to 25th Streets between Harrison and Treat Streets. The first Mission mural was painted in Balmy Alley in 1971, and ever since, nearly every inch has been covered with paint. Much like a traditional gallery, the alley's art is constantly in flux. At any given time, some of the murals will be fading away, some will be works in progress, and others will be at their peak, their colors not yet faded by the elements. Many of Balmy Alley's murals are political, frequently dealing with violence and hunger in Latin America and the gentrification that has driven many low-income people out of the Mission. Several of the murals are painted on garage doors, which residents are usually kind enough to close when visitors come through. Behind the garage door at number 66 is a small gallery called *66balmy,* which features the work of local young artists. Open Thursday and Friday 3:00 to 8:00 P.M., Saturday and Sunday noon to 5:00 P.M. Call 522–0502

See Food

Although it's a bit out of the way in the obscure Excelsior District, a mostly residential area on the southern part of Mission Street, *Joe's Cable Car Restaurant* (4320 Mission Street) may be worth a trip if you truly value a quality hamburger. Several signs outside the restaurant proclaim JOE GRINDS HIS OWN FRESH CHUCK DAILY, an enticement if there ever was one. As if to prove the veracity of this unusual claim, just to the left of the door is a large window, behind which a butcher is busily chopping, weighing, and, yes, grinding meat. Granted, this may gross out vegetarians and those meat eaters who prefer not to think about where their burger is coming from, but these are not Joe's target customers. Joe himself can often be found sitting at one of the few tables doing the finances (not, despite the sign's implications, grinding the chuck himself). By showing the customers exactly what they're getting, Joe is able to set himself apart from the chain burger joints, where the meat can be something of a mystery.

Joe's fiercely loyal clientele would agree, as they sit gleefully munching their burgers, surrounded by murals showing vaguely Eastern European men in various stages of the butchering process. There are sixteen varieties of hamburger offered, each available in a four-, six-, or eight-ounce size. The avocado ground steak burger can't be beat, but you won't go wrong with the original variety either. Since you've made the trip all the way out here anyway, order one of the spectacularly creamy shakes as well. You've earned it, and it's a long trip back to the city's main attractions. Open daily 11:00 A.M. to 11:00 P.M. Call 334–6699 or visit www.joescablecar.com. Inexpensive. At the corner of Mission Street and Silver Avenue. Muni Buses 14, 49, 67.

or visit www.66balmy.com to find out what's on and when you can see it. Phone to verify the location of art on view. The official address is 591 Guerrero Street at 18th Street.

Perhaps the most beloved place of all in the Mission District is slightly out of the neighborhood's main orbit, around 24th Street. About a fifteen-minute walk from that neighborhood center, past the broad Cesar Chavez Street, **Mitchell's Ice Cream** (688 San Jose Avenue at 29th Street) has been San Francisco's essential stop for homemade ice cream since 1943. The shop is still in the Mitchell family, and it still brings in crowds, young and old and from all ethnic groups, to sample their unusual flavors. Many of the concoctions have a Mexican influence, from the luscious mango to the *maize y queso* (corn and cheese), which tastes vaguely like candy corn, and the Mitchells import unusual fruits from the Philippines for exotic tastes like buko, langka, and makapuno. All the choices are made fresh every day, and flavors change with the seasons. Open daily from 11:00 A.M. to 11:00 P.M. Call 648–2300 or visit www.mitchells icecream.com.

To the east and above Mitchell's is Bernal Heights, a small neighborhood of middle-class housing on the side of a steep hill. If you have a car, or if you're feeling particularly hale, head over to Folsom Street and straight up to **Bernal Heights Park,** which is basically a windswept, rocky outcropping with very few trees to obstruct its alarming view. Look down on the lovely houses and steep streets of Noe Valley and the masses of shoppers on Mission Street, then look up at the downtown skyline, the sparkling bay, and all the way across town to the towers of the Golden Gate Bridge. The park is generally less crowded than San Francisco's more mainstream view spots, populated mostly by residents of the immediate neighborhood.

Places to Stay in the Castro and the Mission

Dolores Park Inn
3641 17th Street
621–0482
Well located between the Castro and Mission Districts, and a block from the J-Church Muni Metro streetcar, it can be tough to get a

room in this 1874 Italianate Victorian bed-and-breakfast. The carriage house out back holds a Jacuzzi and the owner's parrot. Moderate.

Inn on Castro
321 Castro Street
861–0321
Very comfortable rooms are available in this quaint, restored Edwardian home. For those who want to stay in the very heart of the Castro, you can't do much better than this. Moderate.

The Inn San Francisco
943 South Van Ness Avenue
641–0188
www.innsf.com
In the heart of the Mission District between 20th and 21st Streets, this beautifully restored 1872 Victorian would command far higher rates in one of the fancier neighborhoods. The rooms range from cramped and cozy to opulent, and there are suites large enough for the whole family. Moderate.

The Parker Guest House
520 Church Street
621–4139
www.parkerguesthouse.com
Another nice Castro area bed-and-breakfast that proudly caters to gay and lesbian travelers and welcomes everyone, The Parker Guest House has twenty-one comfortable, antique-filled rooms, and a library, garden, and steam room. Don't miss the nightly sherry in front of the fire. Moderate.

Places to Eat in the Castro and the Mission

Anchor Oyster Bar
579 Castro Street
431–3990
Bar is the operative word here, because the few tables fill up quickly. Better to sit up near the action anyway, while you're knocking back oyster shooters or sinking into a comfortable bowl of clam chowder. Open Monday through Friday 11:30 A.M. to 10:00 P.M., Saturday noon to 10:00 P.M., Sunday 4:30 to 9:30 P.M. Moderate.

Blue
2337 Market Street
863–2583
The blue and chrome seems trendier-than-thou at first, but then you see the tacky LED display flashing a series of ironic platitudes, and you notice that the stereo is playing cheesy hits of the 1980s like "Eternal Flame" by the Bangles, and Phil Collins's "Don't Lose My Number," and it becomes clear that the place has a sense of humor. Comfort food is the rule, and baked macaroni and cheese and tuna casseroles are house specialties. Open Monday through Thursday 11:30 A.M. to 11:00 P.M., Friday to 11:30 P.M., Saturday 11:00 A.M. to 11:30 P.M., Sunday 11:00 A.M. to 10:00 P.M. Inexpensive.

Dolores Park Cafe
501 Dolores Street
621–2936
www.doloresparkcafe.org
This popular cafe kitty-corner from the park at 18th Street is a good place to refuel with a soup, salad, or sandwich. Sitting outside in San Francisco's sunniest district is a popular weekend activity. Open daily from 7:00 A.M. to 8:00 P.M., and on Friday music nights, from 7:30 to 9:30 P.M. Inexpensive.

Peasant Pies
4108 24th Street
642–1316
www.peasantpies.com
You'll find sweet, fruity pies here, but stop in for the savory pies that fit into the palm of your hand. Whether red potato and leek or spinach, cheese, and mushroom, the flavorful ingredients are baked into a light fluffy crust, making a perfect, concise meal. Open daily 9:30 A.M. to 7:00 P.M.
("Pies are delivered at 10:00 A.M. We are open until pies are sold out.") Inexpensive.

Roosevelt's Tamale Parlor
2817 24th Street
648–2690
Right in the middle of 24th Street, this is the longtime undisputed champ of quality Mexican meals. You can't go wrong with the tamales, juicy marinated pork or chicken surrounded by soft cornmeal and smothered in spicy sauce, rice, beans, and lettuce. On a cold day, top it off with a Mexican chocolate—hot cocoa spiked with cinnamon. Open Tuesday to Saturday 10:00 A.M. to 9:30 P.M., Sunday until 9:00 P.M. Inexpensive.

Walzwerk
381 South Van Ness Avenue
551–7181
www.walzwerk.com
You might have been to a German restaurant, but how about an East German one? Founded by two women who grew up in the DDR state of Thüringer, this place seems to be the real deal, dishing out surprisingly tasty herring and beet dishes accompanied, of course, by a passel of unpronounceable beers. Even the decor looks East German, with black and white shots of smokestacks and the like. Only its obscure location in one of the Mission's grungier blocks keeps this from being a phenomenon. Open Tuesday through Saturday 5:30 to 10:00 P.M. Moderate.

South of Market

The South of Market neighborhood, or SOMA, is, to be blunt, one of San Francisco's least immediately charming areas. Missing are the preserved Victorian homes, the dramatic hillsides, and the rumbling cable cars that come to mind when most people think of the city. This is historically San Francisco's industrial section, originally a low-rent district filled with boardinghouses for single working men. By the end of World War II, SOMA was one of the city's most dangerous neighborhoods, its streets rife with drugs and prostitution, and not much hope was in sight. In the last few decades, however, a flood of redevelopment dollars has begun to transform SOMA, sparking a building boom and the advent of several interesting museums and activity centers. Several more are planned, including an African American Museum of the African Diaspora, scheduled to open in 2005. The Contemporary Jewish Museum and Mexican Museum side-by-side construction of new sites next to St. Patrick's Church may be delayed for lack of funding though visitors will see the foundation in place. The museums followed the lead of the San Francisco Museum of Modern Art in contracting designs by famous architects Daniel Liebeskind and Ricardo Legoretta, respectively.

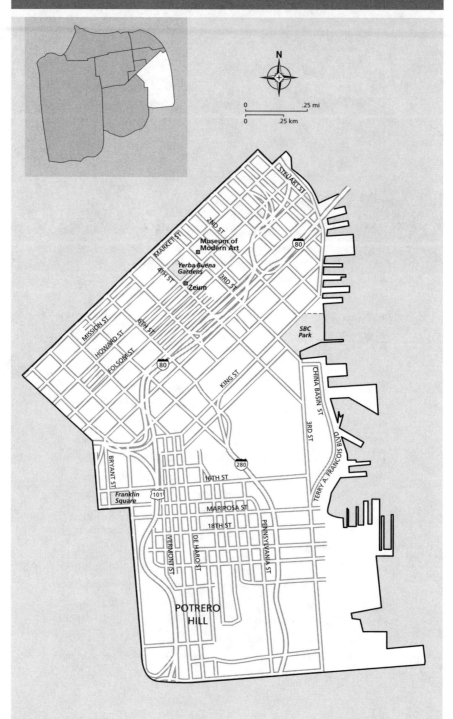

N

0   .25 mi
0   .25 km

STEUART ST

2ND ST

MARKET ST

Museum of
Modern Art

80

Yerba Buena
Gardens

4TH ST

3RD ST

Zeum

MISSION ST

6TH ST

HOWARD ST

SBC
Park

FOLSOM ST

80

KING ST

CHINA BASIN ST

3RD ST

TERRY A. FRANCOIS BLVD

BRYANT ST

280

16TH ST

Franklin
Square

101

MARIPOSA ST

PENNSYLVANIA ST

18TH ST

VERMONT ST

DE HARO ST

POTRERO
HILL

The development hoopla centers around **Yerba Buena Gardens** (Mission Street, between Third and Fourth Streets), which combines much-needed green space for this most urban of areas with a number of popular attractions, including a state-of-the-art movie theater and an ice-skating rink. The chief draw is the nice, big lawn that's perfect for lounging on. As soon as the gardens opened, the many office denizens of the surrounding blocks began taking their lunches here and enjoying the free summer concerts. There are also some interesting public art projects in the gardens, including *Seasons of the Sea Adrift,* by John Roloff, a shiplike structure perched diagonally and partly submerged, with live plants enclosed in the glass hull. Also popular is Terry Allen's *Shaking Man,* a life-size bronze businessman whose repeated features make him appear to be moving.

In the Butterfly Garden, designers planted trees that attract butterflies, and about thirteen different species have been known to show up in the late afternoons. Unfortunately, the trees also attract blackbirds, which like to feast on butterflies. Another section of Yerba Buena Gardens was designed in memory of the Ohlone Indian tribe that once populated the San Francisco peninsula.

Yerba Buena Gardens also holds a thoughtful **Martin Luther King Jr. Memorial,** the largest outside of Atlanta. The design encourages visitors to walk behind a waterfall, where excerpts from the reverend's speeches are engraved in glass panels. The waterfall's symbolism is echoed in the quote from the March on Washington: "No. No, we are not satisfied, and we will not be satisfied until 'justice rolls down like water and righteousness like a mighty stream.'"

Cross the walking bridge over Howard Street and look down to the right to see one of the additions to the Yerba Buena area. The **Carousel at Yerba Buena Gardens** (corner of Howard and 4th Streets) has a long legacy in San Francisco, but it only recently returned after many years of exile. This merry-go-round, populated by camels, giraffes, rams, and horses with real horsehair tails, was hand carved by famed carousel builder Charles Looff in 1906 to be shipped to San Francisco. That year's devastating earthquake and fire temporarily took the city out of the carousel market, so Seattle bought it, erecting

TOP ATTRACTIONS IN SOUTH OF MARKET

Yerba Buena Gardens	Cartoon Art Museum
San Francisco Museum of Modern Art	SBC Park

it in Luna Park. When that amusement center burned down in 1911, the carousel miraculously survived, and it arrived in San Francisco in 1912, where it delighted children at the Playland-at-the-Beach amusement park. Playland closed in 1972, and the carousel spent ten years in limbo followed by—what could be worse?—sixteen years in Los Angeles. In 1998 it was finally shipped back to its true home. Open daily 10:00 A.M. to 6:00 P.M. Call 247–6500 for information or visit www.yerbabuenagardens.com. Rides are $2.00.

The main attraction in the Yerba Buena area is the *San Francisco Museum of Modern Art* (151 Third Street), SFMOMA for short. The museum building, with its distinctive zebra-toned truncated tower, designed by Swiss architect Mario Botta, opened in 1995 and has been jammed with tourists and locals alike ever since. The permanent collection includes works by Robert Rauschenberg, Richard Dienbenkorn, and Man Ray, and dozens of touring exhibitions come through each year. Regular hours are Thursday through Tuesday 11:00 A.M. to 6:00 P.M. The museum stays open until 9:00 P.M. on Thursday night. Widely known as "singles night," this is the essential pickup scene for the cultured crowd. Culture vulture shopaholics raid the extensive and eclectic SFMOMA Museum Store, rated the most-visited museum retail outlet in the United States a few years ago. Admission is $10.00 for adults, $7.00 for seniors, $6.00 for students, free for children ages twelve and under, and half-price Thursday from 6:00 to 9:00 P.M. Free admission the first Tuesday of every month. Call 357–4000 or visit www.sfmoma.org.

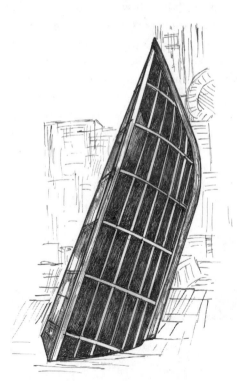

Seasons of the Sea Adrift
by John Roloff

A nice counterpoint to all the modern architecture surrounding Yerba Buena Gardens is *St. Patrick's Church* (756 Mission Street), an 1872 brick structure in the Gothic Revival style. The congregation moved to this spot after first occupying the land on Market Street where the Palace Hotel now stands. The congregation was once entirely Irish but is now mostly Filipino; Sunday mass is

AUTHORS' FAVORITES SOUTH OF MARKET

Yerba Buena Gardens	SBC Park
Cartoon Art Museum	Anchor Brewing Company

celebrated in English and Tagalog. St. Patrick's often hosts free noontime concerts on Wednesday. Call 421–3730.

A block north, the ***Cartoon Art Museum*** (655 Mission Street) pays homage to comic book creators, editorialists, animators, and newspaper strip artists. As the first museum solely devoted to this once-lowbrow art form, it frequently wins the rights to exhibits by major cartoonists, usually featuring rarities like their preliminary sketches. Among the permanent collection are an assortment of early comics-related toys and a room devoted to the unsettling drawings of Edward Gorey. There are also some early Disney sketches that never made it to celluloid. Where else could you find out about Baldie and Jumpy, who did not make the cut when the seven dwarfs were being cast? You'll only need about thirty minutes to take in the Cartoon Art Museum's collection, which makes it a dream for those traveling with kids of all ages, although those older than about ten will get the most out of it. A visit here and a purchase at the gift shop, which features cartoon and comic book collections, might just buy parents a couple of hours at a "legitimate" art museum. Until 2001, this building was occupied by the Ansel Adams Photography Museum, now closed. Half of the gift shop is still devoted to photography books, a number of which feature

Ring My Bells

If you're in the Yerba Buena Gardens on Sunday or other Catholic religious holidays, you're likely to be startled by the reverberating sound of not just one but ten bells echoing off the hotel and office buildings around the area. St. Patrick's Church bells were donated to the important Irish church in 1874 and after the 1906 earthquake they were dug out of earthquake rubble and repaired in West Troy, New York. Organist and choirmaster Steve Repasky discovered a keyboard near the church organ when he arrived in 1986 and found that it connected to the mellifluous bells. Thirty thousand Irish families heard the bells in Victorian times; now, it's Repasky's ten-minute wake-up call and Mass alert for everyone in the neighborhood.

—M.C.

Adams. Open Tuesday through Sunday from 11:00 A.M. to 5:00 P.M. Admission is $6.00 for adults, $4.00 for students and seniors, $2.00 for children ages six to twelve, free for children five and younger; "Pay What You Wish Day" is the first Tuesday of each month. Call 227–8666 or visit www.cartoonart.org.

A winery in San Francisco? *Diablo Grande Wine Gallery* (669 Mission Street), just up the block from the Cartoon Art Museum, has a wine tasting room for its own surprisingly tasty red and white varietals, produced 90 miles east of San Francisco in Stanislaus County's Diablo Foothills. The tasting room serves double duty as a gallery, with exhibits of paintings or photography on the main floor and on the lower level. Tasting costs $5.00 for four wines or $9.00 for eight wines. The cool, sleek sports car near the tasting bar is an Esperante, manufactured by the developer/winery owner's son in Hoschton, Georgia. Open daily 11:00 A.M. to 6:00 P.M. Call 543–4343 or visit www.diablo grande.com.

A fun place for a drink or a quick snack in this part of SOMA is *Eddie Rickenbacker's* (133 Second Street), named for the famous World War I flying ace. Besides downing twenty-six enemy planes and later becoming the chairman of Eastern Airlines, Rickenbacker was also a race car driver, and machines that go fast are the chief decor of the bar. Classic motorcycles fill the windows and clutter the ceiling, hanging low over the bar and tables. Upon request, the bartender will flip the switch that starts a loud electric train rumbling around the room. The crowd during the week is made up mostly of young professionals from the many multimedia businesses in the area, especially at lunchtime and happy hour. Steaks and burgers are the rule, but some lighter

Defenestration

Although SOMA has undergone a renaissance in the last several years, the district still has scads of empty buildings, most of which don't draw much attention. That changed for the building on the corner of Sixth and Howard in 1997, when a local artist, Brian Goggin, turned the lonely brick structure into San Francisco's most eye-catching public art project.

Defenestration, the name of the project, means "the act of throwing a person or thing out of a window." In this case the things in question appear to be throwing themselves out of the top-floor windows. A coffee table, its legs bent in a scurrying motion, hangs far out over the sidewalk, while an armoire, a refrigerator, and a grandfather clock are midway through their escape through other portals. It's not clear just what is inside this building, but whatever it is, it seems to be scaring the dickens out of the furniture. *(Note: The blocks of Sixth Street between Howard and Market Streets are some of the city's most dangerous and should not be walked at night.)*

Defenestration

choices like pastas and salads have been added. Open Monday through Saturday 11:30 to 2:00 A.M. Call 543–3498. Inexpensive.

The ***California Academy of Sciences*** (875 Howard Street), which includes Steinhart Aquarium, Morrison Planetarium, and a natural history museum, moved to temporary quarters in a former department store warehouse in SOMA in 2004. The Indiana Jones–type institution plans to move back to a brand new natural history museum building on the Golden Gate Park Music Concourse, complete with a grass-topped roof, in 2008. In the meantime, many of the critters, crawlers, and Steinhart Aquarium denizens, including an assortment of over-fed alligators, have been farmed out to other institutions for care and feeding. Visitors to the country's oldest scientific institution west of the Rockies, which was founded in 1853, are still amazed by moray eels and snakes—lots of snakes. Emerald boa constrictors and 7-foot-long alligator gars that have lived at the Academy of Sciences since 1947 survived the move. So did penguins, now seen from below and above water. It's a rare chance to see the care of fish from the back of the house as the aquarium tanks are accessible in full view of the public. And those snakes? In SSsssnake Alley, a winding passageway lined with serpents is designed to scare the bravado out of everyone. Open daily 10:00 A.M. to 5:00 P.M. Call 750–7145 or visit www.calacademy.org. Admission is $7.00 for adults, $4.50 for children ages twelve to seventeen, students and seniors, $2.00 for children four to eleven, free for children three and younger.

San Francisco's unpredictable weather patterns can make packing a chore. To ensure yourself comfort throughout your visit, you have to bring several weights of jackets, shirts, and sweaters, all of which clog up a suitcase. But if you run out of clean clothes along the way, don't fret; you now have an excuse to go to **Brain Wash** (1122 Folsom Street), a few blocks southwest of the Yerba Buena Gardens area. Brain Wash is a laundromat, but that fact sometimes gets lost in the shuffle. It is also a cafe, bar, and sometimes club. Sipping a beer and watching a band or a comedian certainly beats watching your clothes spin around the dryer, as mesmerizing as that always is. The food is nothing too fancy, but what more do you want on wash day than a juicy burger or blueberry pancakes? Sitting at one of the wooden tables listing to a jazz combo is nice enough to draw people even without their laundry. You can generally spot the ones doing their wash by their back-of-the-closet attire and the funky diners by their orders of Wash Day Blues (blueberry topped pancakes) or Your Brain on Drugs Egg Sandwiches (spinach included). Open Monday through Thursday 7:00 A.M. to 11:00 P.M., Friday and Saturday to midnight, Sunday 8:00 A.M. to 11:00 P.M. Call 861–3663 or visit www.brainwash.com for the entertainment schedule. Open daily 7:00 A.M. to 11:00 P.M.

It used to be the farther you got from Market Street, the less SOMA had to offer. Going as far south as the area called China Basin meant entering a drab, industrial corner of the city that presented little for the visitor. That all changed in April 2000 with the San Francisco Giants' first game at Pacific Bell Park, now **SBC Park** (King Street between Second and Third Streets). The Giants moved from New York in 1958, and in 1960 they settled into the brand new Candlestick Park, a multipurpose bowl in San Francisco's windswept hinterland. Almost from the first pitch in that lamentable structure south of the city, team owners longed to build a new park closer to the downtown action in a less frigid locale. The China Basin area came up in several stadium plans, but these were usually rejected in public referenda. San Francisco voters were loath to spend their tax dollars on a ballpark. Frustrated owners threatened to pack up the team and move to St. Petersburg, Florida, an idea that outraged the public. A new local ownership group came to the rescue and came up with a plan to build a new ballpark mostly with its own money, a plan the voters heartily approved.

The result is a jewel of a neoclassic ballpark. The facade is mostly brick, and the field has an irregular shape. The seats are right up on the grass, so close that spectators with field-level seats should be warned never to take their eyes off the play, lest they take a foul ball in the snoot. Kids can play beneath an 80-foot-long neon Coca-Cola bottle. The most distinctive thing about the park, however, is its setting, right on the edge of the bay. An inlet is just beyond the right field fence, and the occasional well-struck home run clout can have a wet landing. Consequently, at most games a flotilla of rafts and canoes can be found in the area (named McCovey Cove after Giant hall-of-famer Willie McCovey),

Treasure Island

Midway across San Francisco Bay, the Bay Bridge takes a break, its bed touching down on a pair of islands. To the south of the span is Yerba Buena Island, forested, hilly, and long a natural marker to warn sailors of the shallows to its north. In 1939, just after the bridge was finished, 400 acres of those shallows were filled in, creating **Treasure Island.** Much as the Marina District was built to hold the 1915 Panama Pacific International Exposition, engineers made Treasure Island out of thin water as a home for the Golden Gate International Exposition. Continuing a long San Francisco tradition of changing the landscape to fit the city's needs, Works Progress Administration builders sank 287,000 tons of rock into the shallows, filled in the holes with 20 million cubic yards of sand dredged up from the ocean floor, and topped this off with 50,000 cubic yards of dirt.

These days, Treasure Island doesn't offer much in the way of attractions, except for a fantastic view of the city, day or night.

hoping for a souvenir. When Giant left fielder Barry Bonds was in the midst of breaking his godfather Willie Mays' home run record, so many craft were clogging McCovey Cove that ballpark officials had to ban anything with a motor to make things fairer. Thanks to the efforts of local comedian Father Guido Sarducci (Don Novello), a contingent of Portuguese water dogs are official ball retrievers. Most tickets are sold out well in advance, but the team withholds 500 bleacher seats for sale on game day. For big match-ups, like those against the Oakland Athletics or the hated Los Angeles Dodgers, you'll have to spend the whole day in line to have a chance at one of them. The easiest games to see are the ones played on weekday afternoons, when season ticket holders get stuck at work and often return their tickets to the box office. Even if you get shut out, however, you're not completely out of luck. The right field wall is arcaded, and you can peer through at the game for free. (Ushers will force you to move aside after three innings to give someone else a chance at a free look.) Toting a portable computer? The Giants have a WiFi network in the ballpark to add another distraction from on-field play! Call (510) 762–2277 for ticket information or visit http://sanfrancisco.giants.mlb.com.

Adjacent to SOMA, a ten-minute drive from the ballpark, is **Potrero Hill,** a sometimes forgotten area of the city. Sandwiched between a pair of freeways, it was long a quiet residential and industrial area most famous for giving the world O. J. Simpson. Just below Potrero Hill were shipyards, steel mills, and other industrial concerns. As the SOMA neighborhood has exploded in recent years, however, Potrero Hill's pleasant hilly streets and proximity to the newer places of work have made it one of San Francisco's most desirable neighborhoods to live in. The hill also offers some interesting places for visitors to poke around in.

Few cities are blessed with their own distinctive beer, the one that outsiders may never have tasted but whose very mention evokes thoughts of home for erstwhile residents. San Francisco is lucky enough to have Anchor Steam Beer, made since 1896 by *Anchor Brewing Company* (1705 Mariposa Street). What exactly makes it a "steam beer" is unclear, although company historians say it has something to do with the fact that no ice was used in the

Magical Mystery Tour

If you want to get way off the beaten path, and end up in corners of the city that even the proudest natives haven't seen, you might want to try *Popcorn Anti-Theater.* Part underground art tour, part bacchanalia on wheels, the Popcorn crew assembles once a month on a Potrero Hill street corner, piles a motley bunch onto a tour bus, and embarks on the most bizarre four hours in San Francisco.

I experienced the Popcorn a few nights before Halloween, with plans to play the dispassionate writer, hiding in the corner with my notebook. As soon as I arrived, it was obvious that this was not to be, as the tour's leaders, picking me out as the only one not in costume, had a fellow traveler decorate me with a wig and other accoutrements from a toolbox. It also quickly became apparent that I was probably the only one not somewhat soused, and, wanting to keep with the spirit of the event, I dutifully took a swig from the gallon jug of supermarket whiskey that the tour leader passed around.

Part of the Popcorn thing is that each trip is different, and the guests are never told where they will be taken, but from the outset it was made clear that some of our activities might be illicit. "We occasionally have encounters with the police," our guide said as the bus pulled away. "If the cops come up to you, tell them you are on an art school field trip." He then had us repeat the phrase "art school field trip" like a mantra.

Somewhat disappointingly, we managed to avoid trouble on that evening, but the program was certainly eclectic. We visited a Latino art gallery, walked through a horseshoe court and a backyard with chickens in it to watch a bizarre collage of cheesy black-and-white horror movies, watched an accordion and vocalist duo in one of San Francisco's prime view spots, and rubbed our eyes at a gaggle of mostly naked dancers writhing in the trees of a darkened Golden Gate Park. All in all, not exactly a trip to the Museum of Modern Art or the kind of tour bus trip your grandparents are used to.

When the anarchy of its schedule and whim permits, Popcorn Anti-Theater departs from the corner of 16th and Bryant Streets at 8:00 P.M. Call 695–9100 for information and tickets, about $20. Reservations are essential.

The *Real* Crookedest Street

Forget what you've heard about Lombard Street. Potrero Hill's Vermont Street between 20th and 22nd Streets is the true champion of crookedness, with Lombard coming in second (third, according to the oft-repeated local joke that says Wall Street is the real winner). Take a drive down Vermont, however, and you will quickly see why it has been overshadowed. Missing are the flawless brick roadway, the lovingly maintained flower beds, and the gracious Victorians that delight the throngs on Lombard. The buildings on Vermont are nice, to be sure, but they do not inspire shutter-snapping. Vermont Street is just a street that happens to be curvy.

brewing process in the earliest days. Fritz Maytag of the washing machine and appliance family saved the company from bankruptcy in 1965. Maytag, whose family produced premium Maytag Blue Cheese from a Holstein herd, spearheaded the microbrewery movement in California by reviving the Anchor Steam label and turning a sour, mediocre brew into a prized beverage for beer drinkers. Maytag is now distilling Old Potrero, a 100-percent rye whiskey, an Old Potrero Single Malt Whiskey, and Juniper Gin, as well as pressing olive oil and growing wine grapes in the St. Helena area of the Napa Valley. A visit to the brewery makes for a lovely afternoon. Your guide takes you through the brick chambers to see the brewers stirring pungent vats of wort 20 feet across. The highlight, of course, is the trip to the tasting room, where you'll get to sample not just the steam beer, but the porter, brandywine, and, if you're there in the fall or winter, the famous Christmas Ale, brewed with a different flavor, often spicy, each year. After a visit, you'll start to notice Anchor Brewing Company's blue delivery vans all over the city, your mouth watering in a Pavlovian fashion. Tours can sell out months in advance, so call 863–8350 well ahead of time to make a reservation for the free daily ninety-minute to two-hour tour at 1:00 P.M. or visit www.anchor brewing.com for more information.

The chief commercial stretch on Potrero Hill is 18th Street, and the quintessential hangout is *Farley's* (1315 18th Street), a bright, family-friendly cafe that you'll want to stay in for hours. For starters, the coffee is nice and strong and the pastries are nice and fresh. But people rarely leave when they've swallowed their last bite of English muffin. The magazine rack provides a pleasant distraction, and the pile of board games could keep you busy all day. A tip: When the tables are full on a Sunday morning, don't wait next to a family in the middle of a Monopoly game. Open Monday through Friday 6:30 A.M. to 10:00 P.M., Saturday and Sunday 8:00 A.M. to 10:00 P.M. Call 648–1545. Inexpensive.

Most Potrero Hill establishments are pretty no-nonsense, reflecting the neighborhood's working-class heritage. One joint that puts on airs, however, is ***Lingba Lounge*** ("little monkey lounge") (1469 18th Street), which proudly serves fruit-flavored cocktails with little umbrellas in them. The lights are always low, and the decor tries to evoke Bali for people who will probably never set foot on that island. Nature movies are projected on one wall, perfect for staring at when you can't hear your companion over the DJ's music selection. Sit at the comfortable window seats if you want some intimacy, and share a plate of chicken satay from the adjoining Thai restaurant, Thanya & Salee's. Open daily 5:00 P.M. to 2:00 A.M. Call 355–0001 or visit www.lingba.com.

Places to Stay South of Market

Hotel Griffon
155 Steuart Street
495–2100
www.hotelgriffon.com
The rooms here are charming and relaxing, but the main draw is the view of San Francisco Bay and that other, gray bridge. Beg and plead for a room that overlooks the bay. Moderate.

Hotel Palomar
12 Fourth Street
348–1111
www.hotelpalomar.com
San Franciscans may be as familiar with this boutique hotel's Fifth Floor restaurant, but signature leopard-print room carpeting, specially designed rooms for tall tourists, and pet pampering, complete with a leopard-print doggie bed, take the stuffy out of an urban stay. Proximity to Market Street, Moscone Convention Center,

and the Yerba Buena Gardens and museums doesn't hurt. Expensive.

The Mosser
54 Fourth Street
986–4400
www.themosser.com
Combining Victorian-era charm with modern touches, the Mosser is one of the few affordable hotels so close to downtown, Moscone Convention Center, and Yerba Buena Gardens. Inexpensive.

W San Francisco
181 Third Street
777–5300
www.starwood.com/whotels/
This offshoot of a New York franchise is oh so modern and hip, but also everything you could ask for in a luxury hotel. The hotel has even come up with its own custom-made bed with a "pillow-top" mattress. W San Francisco is convenient to the Yerba Buena area and the Financial District. Expensive.

Places to Eat South of Market

Julie's Supper Club
1123 Folsom Street
861–0707
www.juliessupperclub.com
Hearty dishes are served in a swinger atmosphere that's a throwback to the fifties. Join the after-work crowd for a martini at the bar, then retreat to the Marlin Room for a pork chop. A fun spot on one of SOMA's more happening blocks. Open Tuesday through Thursday 5:00 to 10:30 P.M., Friday and Saturday until 11:00 P.M.; closed Sunday and Monday. Moderate.

Natoma Café
145 Natoma Street
495–3289
Wander behind SFMOMA to this unadorned breakfast and lunch spot that makes an ethnic melting pot of dishes—all well—from Greek mint salad, a challah bread

sandwich with ham, pineapple, and cheddar cheese, Tuscan pasta, to a Burmese noodle feast. Imaginative soup choices include lentil, complementing locally named vegetarian sandwiches: Mario Botta, after SFMOMA's architect; South Beach after a trendy oval-shaped SOMA park; Hotel W; and Yerba Buena. Open Monday through Friday 7:00 A.M. to 4:00 P.M. Inexpensive.

The Ramp

855 China Basin Street (Terry Francois Boulevard) 621–2378
This waterfront restaurant is a sun-worshipper's delight. Sit on the huge patio under one of the umbrellas with beer ads on them and enjoy a leisurely brunch, lunch, or dinner. Set in what was once solely an industrial area one mile south of SBC Park, The Ramp is a favorite of the young SOMA set. Open Monday through Friday 11:00 A.M. to 10:00 P.M., Saturday and Sunday 9:00 A.M. to 8:30 P.M. Muni Buses 15, 22. Moderate.

Rocco's Cafe

1131 Folsom Street
554–0522
There's nothing fancy about Rocco's. This is old-time Italian food of the linguine-in-clam-sauce variety done to perfection. The place is lively and comfortable, with a loyal lunchtime crowd. No matter how rough the morning was, the gnocchi in pesto sauce seems to raise their spirits for the afternoon. Open Monday and Tuesday 7:00 A.M. to 3:00 P.M., Wednesday through Friday to 10:00 P.M., Saturday 8:00 A.M. to 10:00 P.M., Sunday 8:00 A.M. to 4:00 P.M. Inexpensive.

Thirsty Bear Brewing Company

661 Howard Street
974–0905
www.thirstybear.com
The convention crowd, after-work barflies, and folks who spent the day enjoying Yerba Buena Gardens and nearby museums find this brewpub and tapas restaurant conducive to making contact with like minds. Metal-braced, red brick former warehouse walls were converted to a high and noisy space, with the restaurant in the back separated from the large, golden-lit bar area. The nine beers on tap include Polar Bear and Brown Bear Ales and fresh firkin kegs of cask-conditioned ales tapped every Tuesday at 5:30 P.M. Spanish dishes like *sopa del ajo* (garlic soup), *embutidos* (cured Spanish cold cuts), *kokotxas* (sherry garlic sauce covers fish cheeks), and *bacalaoditos* (a salt cod sandwich) make share-around snacks an ice-breaker. Sunday nights are for flamenco at 7:15 and 8:45 P.M., with a prix fixe menu offered to supplement the dinner menu. Open Monday through Thursday 11:30 A.M. to 11:00 P.M., Friday and Saturday to 12:30 A.M., Sunday 4:30 to 10:30 P.M. Moderate.

Appendix

Top Five San Francisco Experiences

Sipping coffee in North Beach
A Giants game at SBC Park
Watching the hang gliders at Fort Funston
Picnicking at the Palace of Fine Arts
Hanging off the side of the Powell-Hyde Cable Car

Bottom Five San Francisco Experiences

Muni breakdowns
Sudden temperature changes
The Powell Street Cable Car Turnaround
Parking
Earthquakes

Places Kids Will Love and Parents Won't Hate

Randall Museum
Japanese Tea Garden
Cartoon Art Museum
Yerba Buena Gardens
The Exploratorium

Best Places to Get Religion

Grace Cathedral
Glide Memorial Church
Temple Emanu-El
Saints Peter and Paul Church
Fishermen's and Seamen's Memorial Chapel

Natural Highs

Fort Funston
Glen Park Canyon
The Presidio
Golden Gate Park
Sutro Baths

Best Shopping Streets

Hayes Street (Civic Center)
Clement Street (the Richmond)
Union Street (Cow Hollow)
Stockton Street (Chinatown)
24th Street (the Mission, Noe Valley)

Best Bookstores

City Lights
Black Oak Books
Green Apple
Stacey's

Best Streets for Nightlife

Columbus Avenue (North Beach)
Union Street (Cow Hollow)
Valencia Street (the Mission)
Castro Street (the Castro)

Best International Neighborhoods

Italian (North Beach)
Chinese (Chinatown, the Richmond)
Mexican and Central American (the Mission)
French (Union Square)

Best Places to See Free Art

San Francisco Art Institute
Coit Tower
Beach Chalet
Presidio Chapel

Indexes

GENERAL INDEX

Absinthe, 14
African Outlet, The, 10
Albion House Inn, 14
Alta Plaza Park, 98
Ambassador Toys, 58
Amoeba Music, 89
Anchor Brewing Company, 128–29
Anchor Oyster Bar, 117
Angel Island, 48
Appendix, 133–34
Aquarium of the Bay, 44
Aquatic Park, 47
Archbishop's Mansion Inn, The, 100
Arlequin, 15
Asian Art Museum, 6
Audium, 97

Balmy Alley, 115
Bambuddha Lounge, 12
Bank of California, 24
Bank of California Museum, 23–24
Beach Chalet, 73
Beach Chalet Brewery &
  Restaurant, 74
Beanery, The, 81–82
Bella, 84–85
Bernal Heights Park, 116
Bimbo's 365 Club, 49–50
Black Oak Books, 81
Blue, 117
Brain Wash, 126
Buena Vista Park, 90, 92
Buffalo Paddock, 75

Cable Car Barn, 32–33
Cafe du Nord, 109–10
Cafe Flore, 109
Café Niebaum-Coppola, 50
Caffe Sport, 50–51
Caffe Trieste, 40
California Academy of
  Sciences, 77, 125

Canvas Cafe and Gallery, 80
Carousel at Yerba Buena
  Gardens, 121
Cartoon Art Museum, 123
Castro Camera, 106
Castro District, 105–10
Castro Theatre, 108
Catnip+bones, 60
Cha! Cha! Cha!, 100
Champ de Mars, 10
Chestnut Street, 60–61
Chinatown, 25–27
City Hall, 1–5
City Lights Bookstore, 39
Cliff's Variety, 107
Coit Tower, 43
Conservatory of Flowers, 78
Corona Heights, 103–5
Corazon de la Mission, 114
Cow Hollow, 53–58

Davies Symphony Hall, 9
Day's Inn, 84
de Young Museum, 77
de Young Art Center, 83
Defenestration, 124
Diablo Grande Wine Gallery, 124
Dolores Park, 111–12
Dolores Park Cafe, 117
Dolores Park Inn, 116
Dolphin Club, 47

Ebisu, 80–81
Eddie Rickenbacker's, 124–25
Edinburgh Castle, 14
Edward II Inn & Suites, 68
Eight Immortals, 85
El Farolito, 114
Eliza's, 101
Embarcadero, The, 20
Empire Park, 25
Eos, 101

Espetus, 15
Exploratorium, 62–63

Farley's, 129
Ferry Building, 17
Ferry Plaza Farmers Market, 19–20
Filbert Steps, 44
Fillmore Auditorium, 94–95
Financial District, 17–24
Fire Department Museum, 99
First Bank, 24
Fisherman's Wharf, 44–47
Fishermen's and Seamen's
    Chapel, 45–46
Folk Art International, 29
Foreign Cinema, 112–13
Fort Funston, 83–84
Fort Mason, 59–60
Fort Point National Historic
    Site, 66–67
Four Seas, 34
Frjtz, 11

Glide Memorial Church, 13
Golden Gate Park, 73–78
Golden Gate Park Visitor's Center, 73
Grace Cathedral, 31
Great American Music Hall,
    The, 12
Great Highway Inn, 84
Green Street Mortuary Band, 49
Greens Restaurant, 59
Greens to Go, 60
Grove, The, 61

Haight-Ashbury, 87–92
Harry Bridges Plaza, 20
Harvey Milk Civil Rights
    Academy, 106
Harvey Milk Plaza, 105–6
Harvey's, 107
Hayes and Vine Wine Bar, 10
Hayes Street Grill, 15
Hayes Valley, 9–12
Hayes Valley Inn, 14
Herbst Theater, 7

Holy Trinity Russian Cathedral, 53
Hotei, 81
Hotel Astoria, 33
Hotel Boheme, 50
Hotel del Sol, 68
Hotel Drisco, 100
Hotel Griffon, 130
Hotel Huntington, 33
Hotel Palomar, 130
Hotel Triton, 33
Huntington Park, 31–32

Inn at the Opera, 14
Inn on Castro, 116
Inn San Francisco, The, 116
Irish Bank, The, 30–31
Isobune, 101

Jack's Record Cellar, 92
Jackson Fillmore, 98
Japan Center, 95–96
Japanese Tea Garden, 75–76
Java Beach, 85
Joe's Cable Car Restaurant, 115
John Lee Hooker's Boom Boom
    Room, 94
John's Grill, 26
Julie's Supper Club, 130

Le Video, 80
Lefty O'Doul's, 29–30
Levi Strauss Factory, 112
Levi's Store, 28
Liguria Bakery, 42
Lincoln Park, 71
Lingba Lounge, 130
Little Shamrock, the, 77
Liverpool Lil's, 68
Lloyd Lake, 75
Lotta's Fountain, 21
Lower Haight, 92–93
Lucca Delicatessen, 61
Lucca Ravioli Company, 113

Mad Dog in the Fog, 92
Magnolia Pub & Brewery, 101

Maiden Lane, 28–29
Main Post, 63
Maltese Falcon, The, 26
Marco Polo, 85
Marina District, the, 60–64
Mario's Bohemian Cigar Store Cafe, 51
Marnee Thai, 82
Martin Luther King Jr. Memorial, 121
Max's Opera Cafe, 15
Medium Rare Records, 108–9
Metro Hotel, The, 100
Mission Basilica, 111
Mission District, 110–16
Mission San Francisco de Asis
    (Mission Dolores), 110–11
Mitchell's Ice Cream, 116
Molinari's Delicatessen, 51
Momi Toby's Revolution Cafe, 11
Mosser, The, 130
Mount Davidson, 84
Music Concourse, 76

National AIDS Memorial Grove, 77
Natoma Café, 130–31
Next-to-New Shop, 98
Nob Hill, 31–32
North Beach Museum, 37
North (Dutch) Windmill, 74

Octagon House, 55–56
Old Saint Mary's, 27
Orchard Hotel, The, 33

Pacific Heights, 97–99
Palace of Fine Arts, 61–62
Palace of the Legion of Honor, 71–72
Park Chalet Garden Restaurant, 74
Park Chow, 85
Parker Guest House, The, 117
Peasant Pies, 117
Perry's, 57
Phoenix Hotel, 14
Pier 45, 45
Pluto's, 85
Popcorn Anti-Theater, 128
Portals of the Past, 75

Portsmouth Square, 26–27
Post Chapel, 65
Potrero Brewing Company, 128–29
Potrero Hill, 127–28
Prayerbook Cross, 83
Precita Eyes Mural Arts Center,
    114–15
Presidio, The, 63–66
Presidio Pet Cemetery, 67

Queen Anne Hotel, 96
Queen Wilhelmina Tulip Garden, 75

Radisson Miyako Hotel, 100
Ramp, The, 131
Randall Museum, 103
Red Victorian Bed, Breakfast, and
    Art, The, 89–90
Refugee Huts, 64
Repeat Performance, 98
Richmond District, 69–71
Rocco's Cafe, 131
Roosevelt's Tamale Parlor, 117
Rose's Cafe, 68

Saints Peter and Paul Church, 42
Sam's Grill, 34
San Francisco Art Institute, 49
San Francisco Brewing Company, 38
San Francisco Columbarium, 91
San Francisco Maritime Museum, 48
San Francisco Maritime National
    Historic Park, 47
San Francisco Museum of Modern
    Art, 122
San Francisco Public Library, 5–6
San Francisco War Memorial, 6–7
San Remo Hotel, 50
SBC Park, 126–27
Schroeder's, 34
Seal Rock Inn, 84
Sherman House, 56–57
66balmy, 115–16
South End Rowing Club, 47
South (Murphy) Windmill, 75
Southern Pacific Building, 23

St. John Coltrane African Orthodox
Church, 95
St. Patrick's Church, 122–23
Stanyan Park Hotel, 100
Steps of Rome, 40
Stern Grove, 82
Stockton Street, 27
Stow Lake, 75
Sunset Supermarket, 82
Sunset District, 78–84
Suppenküche, 15
Sutro Baths, 72

Tadich Grill, 34
Tel-Aviv Strictly Kosher Meats, 82
Telegraph Hill, 42–43
Temple Emanu-El, 69
Tenderloin, the, 12–13
Thirsty Bear Brewing Company, 131
Tinhorn Press, 12
Toland Hall, 78–79
Tosca Cafe, 40
Treasure Island, 127
24th Street, 114
Twin Peaks, 108

U.S. Restaurant, 51
U-Lee, 51
Union Square, 27–28
Union Street, 57–58
Union Street Inn, 68

USS *Pampanito,* 46–47
USS *San Francisco* Memorial, 71

Vedanta Temple, 58
Vesuvio Cafe, 38
Veterans Building, 7
Vicolo Pizzeria, 15
Visitor Information Center
(Presidio), 63
Volunteer Fire Fighters
Memorial, 41–42

W San Francisco, 130
Walzwerk, 117
War Memorial Opera House, 8–9
Warming Hut, 65–66
Washington Square, 40
Washington Square Inn, 50
Wave Organ, 63
Wells Fargo History Museum, 21–23
Western Addition, 93–97
Western Terminus of the Pony
Express, 25
Wharf Inn, The, 50
World Famous Sears Fine Food, 30

Xanadu Gallery, 29

Yerba Buena Gardens, 121–23

Zuni Cafe, 15

RESTAURANTS

Absinthe, 14
Anchor Oyster Bar, 117
Arlequin, 15
Bambuddha Lounge, 12
Beach Chalet Brewery &
Restaurant, 74
Beanery, The, 81–82
Bella, 84
Blue, 117
Brain Wash, 126
Cafe du Nord, 109–10
Cafe Flore, 109

Café Niebaum-Coppola, 50
Caffe Sport, 50–51
Caffe Trieste, 40
Canvas Cafe and Gallery, 80
Cha! Cha! Cha!, 100
Dolores Park Cafe, 117
Ebisu, 80–81
Eddie Rickenbacker's, 124–25
Eight Immortals, 85
El Farolito, 114
Eliza's, 101
Eos, 101

Espetus, 15
Farley's, 129
Four Seas, 34
Foreign Cinema, 112–13
Frjtz, 11
Greens Restaurant, 59
Greens to Go, 60
Grove, The, 61
Harvey's, 107
Hayes and Vine Wine Bar, 10
Hayes Street Grill, 15
Hotei, 81
Irish Bank, The, 30–31
Isobune, 101
Jackson Fillmore, 98
Java Beach, 85
Joe's Cable Car Restaurant, 115
John's Grill, 26
Julie's Supper Club, 130
Lefty O'Doul's, 29–30
Liverpool Lil's, 68
Magnolia Pub & Brewery, 101
Mario's Bohemian Cigar Store Cafe, 51
Marnee Thai, 82
Max's Opera Cafe, 15

Molinari's Delicatessen, 51
Momi Toby's Revolution Cafe, 11
Natoma Café, 130–31
Park Chow, 85
Peasant Pies, 117
Perry's, 57
Pluto's, 85
Ramp, The, 131
Rocco's Cafe, 131
Roosevelt's Tamale Parlor, 117
Rose's Cafe, 68
Sam's Grill, 34
San Francisco Brewing Company, 38
Schroeder's, 34
Steps of Rome, 40
Suppenküche, 15
Tadich Grill, 34
Thirsty Bear Brewing Company, 131
U.S. Restaurant, 51
U-Lee, 51
Vicolo Pizzeria, 15
Walzwerk, 117
Warming Hut, 65–66
World Famous Sears Fine Food, 30
Zuni Cafe, 15

LODGINGS

Albion House Inn, 14
Archbishop's Mansion Inn, The, 100
Day's Inn, 84
Dolores Park Inn, 116
Edward II Inn & Suites, 68
Great Highway Inn, 84
Hayes Valley Inn, 14
Hotel Astoria, 33
Hotel Boheme, 50
Hotel del Sol, 68
Hotel Drisco, 100
Hotel Griffon, 130
Hotel Huntington, 33
Hotel Palomar, 130
Hotel Triton, 33
Inn at the Opera, 14
Inn on Castro, 116
Inn San Francisco, The, 116

Metro Hotel, The, 100
Mosser, The, 130
Orchard Hotel, The, 33
Parker Guest House, The, 117
Phoenix Hotel, 14
Queen Anne Hotel, 96
Radisson Miyako Hotel, 100
Red Victorian Bed, Breakfast, and
   Art, The, 89–90
San Remo Hotel, 50
Seal Rock Inn, 84
Sherman House, 56–57
Stanyan Park Hotel, 100
Union Street Inn, 68
W San Francisco, 130
Washington Square Inn, 50
Wharf Inn, The, 50

About the Authors

Michael Petrocelli was born and raised just to the north of San Francisco in the small town of Mill Valley. He holds a bachelor's degree in history from the University of California at Berkeley, just east of the great city, and he earned a master's in journalism from Columbia University. He currently works as a newspaper reporter in North Carolina, where he misses San Francisco each and every day.

Maxine Cass was born on the Stanford University campus in Palo Alto when the area was "The Valley of Heart's Delight," long before Silicon Valley loomed. She grew up in and around San Francisco. At the age of seventeen, she went south to the University of California, Santa Barbara, to discover a wide world while earning a dual degree in history and Medieval studies. After a stint in the Peace Corps in Senegal, West Africa, she returned to San Francisco, where she has worked as a freelance writer, photographer, and guidebook writer for more than two decades.